Acclaim for *And You Will Find Rest*

"My copy of *And You Will Find Rest* is well-worn. It first served as a wonderful companion on a retreat led by Fr. Sattler and has since been a trusted reference for the wisdom of the great Spanish spiritual masters, St. Teresa of Ávila and St. John of the Cross. Having lived in solitude as a hermit for many years as well as having served as a beloved shepherd of souls, Fr. Sattler is uniquely positioned to open contemporary eyes to the insights of the great Carmelite mystics in a way that leads us into the mystery of contemplative prayer and the beauty of a life lived in union with the God who loves us first."

—***Archbishop Bernard Hebda,***
Archdiocese of Saint Paul & Minneapolis

"With the reprinting of *And You Will Find Rest,* Fr. Sattler's wonderful guide to live in prayer with the Lord will be available to many more persons in their quest for a deep relationship with God. Drawing upon the richness of the lives and the prayers of Sts. John of the Cross and Teresa of Ávila, Fr. Sattler offers us a simple yet profound guide to govern our own prayer and to deepen it so that we may not only converse with the Lord but, more importantly, allow Him in the silence of our heart to converse with us as our intimate and best Friend. This is a book everyone should read and keep at hand. As his bishop, I not only recommend this book but also use it for meditation in my daily holy hour."

—***Bishop David Kagan,*** Diocese of Bismarck

"Having known Fr. Sattler for over thirty years, I can attest that what has been written has been practiced. This scholarly yet practical guide to a life of prayer will both challenge and encourage the reader to move forward in a faith-filled and loving relationship with God. Fr. Sattler offers an understanding of the best of the Carmelite tradition of contemplative prayer. I would encourage all desiring a serious prayer life to delve deeply into this contemporary classic."

—***Bishop David L. Toups,*** Diocese of Beaumont

"This book is an arrow of truth and light challenging us to acknowledge and experience the true nature of God as it is revealed in prayer, a nature wildly compassionate and beautiful and loving and yet always somehow demanding. This is a work that speaks to all of us. It is remarkable in the way it lays bare with such gentle yet unsparing clarity the loving, purifying stages of the journey into God as described by Sts. Teresa of Ávila and John of the Cross. From start to finish, the work has the quality of a personal testimony. Its author is a man of prayer who has clearly experienced the shock of grace, the knowledge, that is, not only of what we ourselves are called to do in the spiritual life but, more importantly, the knowledge of all that God is doing for us at every moment in the life of prayer. This is a treasure of a book, a work to be lived with and prayed with."

—***Fr. Paul Murray, O.P.,*** Professor Emeritus, The Angelicum

"Even for the committed believer, prayer can be a daunting experience. What am I supposed to do when I pray? What if I don't feel anything? What difference does it really make? With St. John of the Cross and St. Teresa of Ávila as his guides, Fr. Wayne Sattler not only makes contemplative prayer understandable, but he presents it as something we do not want to live without. *And You Will Find Rest* is a spiritual gem, which will remind every reader of God's desire for each one of us: 'Remain in my love' (John 15:9)."

—***Msgr. Thomas Powers,*** Rector,
The Pontifical North American College

"*And You Will Find Rest* helpfully and insightfully integrates the sometimes difficult, but important, works of two heroes of the Catholic spiritual life — Sts. Teresa of Ávila and John of the Cross. Combining lived experience with deep spiritual truths, Fr. Sattler makes the mysticism of these great saints accessible and attractive, with all the robust features of the Carmelite tradition. A fruitful read!"

—***Msgr. James P. Shea,*** President, University of Mary

"We have benefited from Fr. Sattler's personal instruction in our Diaconate Formation Program over the past two decades. In simple terms, Fr. Sattler opens up a path we can take to understanding the great mystics, St. Teresa of Ávila and St. John of the Cross, by unifying their respective experiences of prayer. Through this complementary lens, the reader cannot help but grow in desire to be in union with God here and now, and ultimately for all eternity!"

—***Dcn. David Fleck,*** Director, Office of the Diaconate for the Diocese of Bismarck

"After reading *And You Will Find Rest,* I was deeply moved by its profound insights into what God does during prayer. As a library specialist, I felt compelled to share a book review in the library newsletter, encouraging others to read the book. Fr. Sattler writes in clear, concise language and with text that is easy to comprehend and engage with. I recommend this title to all Christians — not only Catholics — who are interested in experiencing a profound prayer life and a deeper relationship with God."

—***Kathy Cline,*** Library Specialist

"This book will change your life. As a wife and mother, the wisdom and guidance on these pages allowed me to know God's love more deeply and to understand what purification and dryness in prayer can look like. In a society where we strive to achieve and being uncomfortable can be seen as failure, it is freeing to understand how God is wanting us to grow more deeply in those frustrating seasons instead of giving up and feeling that a deeply spiritual life is for someone 'more holy.' This book will open your heart and mind to the gift of prayer and reveal how a deep prayer life is there for all souls, not only those living in religious communities. Fr. Sattler has a gift of sharing deeply profound wisdom in such a clear and simple way that will speak to all souls no matter where they are in their journey."

—***Dr. Elizabeth Jones,*** Founder and Owner, Jones Physical Therapy

AND YOU WILL FIND REST

Fr. Wayne Sattler

AND YOU WILL FIND REST

What God Does in Prayer

Based on the writings of St. Teresa of Ávila and St. John of the Cross

SOPHIA INSTITUTE PRESS
Manchester, New Hampshire

And You Will Find Rest: What God Does in Prayer was previously published in 2020 by the University of Mary Press, Bismark, ND. This 2024 edition contains minor revisions and updates by the author.

Cover by LUCAS Art & Design, Jenison, MI
Cover image: *Philosopher in Contemplation* by Rembrandt

Sophia Institute Press
Box 5284, Manchester, NH 03108
1-800-888-9344
www.SophiaInstitute.com

Sophia Institute Press is a registered trademark of Sophia Institute.

paperback ISBN 979-8-88911-482-6

ebook ISBN 979-8-88911-483-3

Library of Congress Control Number: 2024945950

First printing

Special thanks to Karen Herzog and Joanie Agamenoni for their generous and painstaking review of this text.

Nihil Obstat & Imprimatur

The Most Reverend David D. Kagan, D.D., P.A., J.C.L.
Bishop of Bismarck
March 19, 2020

The *Nihil Obstat and Imprimatur* are official declarations that a book is considered to be free of doctrinal or moral error. No implication is contained therein that those who have granted the *Nihil Obstat* or the *Imprimatur* agree with the contents, opinions, or statements expressed.

Take my yoke upon you and learn from me . . .
And you will find rest.

– Matthew 11:29

Contents

AND YOU WILL FIND REST

Introduction

If you were to search on the Internet for "The Dark Night of the Soul," you would be misled by many of the references. On the very first page it would be described as "spiritual depression," "a kind of existential crisis." An explanation is given "that anyone may go through a period of sadness or challenge that is so deep-seated and tenacious that it qualifies as the dark night of the soul." The search would stray so far afield as to reference the 2008 movie about Batman, *The Dark Knight*. Even the seemingly safe accreditation as the title of a book written by St. John of the Cross still doesn't get it quite right.

For the record, "The Dark Night of the Soul" is not the title of a book written by St. John of the Cross. The poem he wrote to describe the experience of what God does in prayer to prepare a soul for union with Him is entitled "The Dark Night." The explanation he later wrote for this poem is divided into two parts. The first part St. John refers to as "The Dark Night of the Senses." Here he explains how the senses of our soul are purified by God to accommodate them to the spirit, where His gift of contemplation is received. The second part St. John refers to as "The Dark Night of the Spirit (or Soul)." Here he explains how the spirit is purified by God to accommodate it for union with Him. So "The Dark Night of the Soul" is the second part of a commentary St. John wrote to explain his poem "The Dark Night."

St. John of the Cross

Francisco de Zurbarán (1598–1664)

Museum of Katowice Archdiocese
Cathedral of Christ the King, Katowice, Poland

The first part, "The Dark Night of the Senses," is described as "common and happens to many."[1] The second part, "The Dark Night of the Spirit (or Soul)," "is the lot of very few, those who have been tried and are proficient."[2]

He is most intent on explaining what happens in the second part, "The Dark Night of the Spirit (or Soul)." "For hardly anything has been said of it, in sermons or in writing, and even the experience of it is rare."[3] This remains true five hundred years later. In fact, today, hardly anything even seems to be said of the first part, "The Dark Night of the Senses."

St. Teresa of Ávila expresses the same concern in the beginning of her work *The Interior Castle.* She explains to her sisters that "we always hear about what a good thing prayer is; our constitutions [their Carmelite religious community rule of life] oblige us to spend many hours in prayer. Yet only what we ourselves can do in prayer is explained to us; little is explained about what the Lord does in a soul, I mean about the supernatural."[4]

St. John of the Cross and St. Teresa of Ávila were both members of the Carmelite religious order in Spain during the sixteenth century. In the Catholic Church, religious orders are recognized as either "active" or "contemplative." Active religious orders carry out an apostolate, like teaching or caring for the sick, as a fruit of their life of prayer. Contemplative religious orders are structured to avail themselves more fully to the work of God in prayer, drawing them and the

1 St. John of the Cross, *The Collected Works of St. John of the Cross,* trans. Kieran Kavanaugh, O.C.D. and Otilio Rodriguez, O.C.D. (Washington, D.C.: ICS, 1973), *The Dark Night,* bk. 1, chap. 8, par. 1.

2 Ibid.

3 Ibid., par. 2.

4 St. Teresa of Ávila, *The Collected Works of St. Teresa of Ávila, Volume Two,* trans. Kieran Kavanaugh, O.C.D. and Otilio Rodriguez, O.C.D. (Washington, D.C.: ICS, 1980), *The Interior Castle,* dwelling 1, chap. 2, par. 7.

world they pray for into union with Him. The Carmelites in Spain during the sixteenth century were a contemplative religious order struggling to maintain that clear focus on their life of prayer. St. John and St. Teresa came to understand very well how even good contemplative religious community members, who commit themselves to a life of prayer, do not always appreciate what God is doing in prayer.

Contemplation is generally regarded as the height and goal of Christian prayer. Yet there is much confusion surrounding the method and meaning of contemplation, even in Christian circles.

It is helpful to realize that the word *contemplation* is built upon two Latin words: *con* and *templum*.

- ✠ *Con,* meaning "with,"
- ✠ *Templum,* defined as "a sacred space cut off."
- ✠ A good English derivative of *templum* is the word "temple."

Contemplation serves to mark that point in prayer when what is being experienced is no longer merely the activity of man, but the pure activity of God.

Contemplation is what God does in prayer.

It is a distinction missed by many; particularly, it seems, by those trying to teach others to pray. It was a distinction being missed among the Carmelites in Spain in the sixteenth century.

Shortly after his ordination as a priest in the Carmelite Order, St. John of the Cross was seriously considering a transfer to the Carthusian Order. The Carthusians had remained true to their own contemplative vocation. By the time St. John was ordained a priest, St. Teresa was already working hard on reforming the female branch of the Carmelites in Spain. She arranged for a meeting with St. John to seek his assistance in extending her plan of reform to the male branch of the Spanish Carmelites. It was the fall of 1568; she was

St. Teresa of Ávila

Peter Paul Rubens (1577–1640)

Kunsthistorisches Museum
Vienna, Austria

fifty-two and he was twenty-five. The rest of their lives would be spent on this reform.

As promised by Our Lord, they would be "hated by all" (Matt. 10:22). St. Teresa once pondered if anyone would hear her confession because of the gossip being spread that she was trying to make herself out to be a saint. Some considered her as a soul gone astray; even those she considered friends turned away from her.[5] St. John was at one time excommunicated, imprisoned by his own religious brothers, and locked up in a six-by-ten-foot closet, apparently for life. In the midst of such discouraging conditions, they learned in prayer how to accept Our Lord's invitation to "take my yoke upon you and learn from me ... and you will find rest" (Matt. 11:29). A rest, which Pope Benedict XVI recognizes, is not the same as an absence of conflict.[6] It is the rest Our Lord extends to those who "labor and are burdened" (Matt. 11:28), to those who have realized that "in the world you will have trouble" (John 16:33), yet, by entering "into His yoke" and "learning from Him," go forward in the truth Jesus assures us, that He has "conquered the world" (John 16:33). In that yoke, St. John came to observe how this path that seems "so rough and adverse and contrary to spiritual gratification engenders so many blessings."[7] For the rest that God gives us is a peace the world cannot give (John 14:27), "a peace beyond understanding" (Phil. 4:7), a peace Pope Benedict XVI recognizes as "the result of a constant battle against evil,"[8] a peace that despite all the turmoil St. John would encounter, enabled him to recognize, at a much deeper level, his "house being now all stilled."[9]

5 Ibid., 6.1.3–4.

6 Benedict XVI, Angelus (August 19, 2007).

7 St. John of the Cross, *The Dark Night*, 1.11.4.

8 Benedict XVI, Angelus (August 19, 2007).

9 St. John of the Cross, *The Dark Night*, 1.13.15.

The path to this stillness, this rest, is one the Church directs us toward in declaring both St. John and St. Teresa as Doctors of the Church. St. John, in particular, is referred to as the Mystical Doctor of the Church.

Our first approach to the Mystical Doctor of the Church isn't what we might expect. We could assume that he would mark off some precise steps on how to advance toward the goal of contemplation. This poet of five centuries ago, reflecting on what begins to occur in a soul that is set on loving God for the sake of God alone, may come as a surprise. Far from providing a clear path on how to aggressively advance in holiness, "The Dark Night" describes the rather lovesick experience of a soul who can only find its rest in God, proving once again that it is the sick who are in need of a doctor (Matt. 9:12).

Our first attempt to read his writings can prove more than we are ready to digest. That isn't meant to discourage us from ever being fed by him. His texts are not meant to be a onetime read. We will not be able to simply breeze through them.

There can be a danger in being introduced too early to the person most capable of helping us, encountering them at a time in our life when we aren't really looking for any assistance. If you have tried to read St. John of the Cross and found it difficult, do not be discouraged. Proper timing and experience of life will play a large factor in appreciating his wisdom — wisdom to carry with us along the journey, not to read through just once.

I remember carrying a copy of *The Collected Works of St. John of the Cross* as I boarded the plane to begin my theological seminary studies in Rome. I definitely did not understand everything he wrote, but what I could understand spoke very deeply.

Eleven years later, I read through *The Dark Night* in its entirety for the first time. In fact, I read through it during the course of one day. I laughed, I cried, and was confirmed in ways words cannot explain on what God had been doing in my soul for the past eight or nine years.

The following year, I spent thirty days with a small group of Carmelite hermits to discern my own persistent call to a contemplative vocation. During that time, the inspiration came to draft a retreat on *The Dark Night*. I had given a few retreats to religious communities and taught some classes in our diocesan permanent diaconate formation program. From that moment on, the material would be on *The Dark Night*.

In that poem, St. John describes how on this path of purification that leads to union with God, he had "no other light than the one that burned in my heart. That guided me more surely than the light of noon to where He was awaiting me."[10] In my own discernment of a call to a contemplative vocation, I visited numerous religious communities. In that process of discernment, I became acquainted with a unique expression of the contemplative vocation as a diocesan hermit. Hermits typically live in the midst of a contemplative religious community where they are able to receive guidance from other hermits. The 1983 Code of Canon Law opened the door for one to live alone as a hermit while under the direction of the diocesan bishop.

In June of 2006, after years of discernment with my bishop, I was given permission to live as a diocesan hermit. For the next six years, I settled into a one-room cabin on an abandoned farmstead in rural North Dakota. It was far from the six-by-ten-foot closet in which St. John was imprisoned. Yet it was in this space that the material on *The Dark Night* continued to be fleshed out. As a diocesan hermit, there would be no other guide than the one that burned in my heart. Quite

[10] St. John of the Cross, *The Dark Night*, prologue for reader, stanzas of the soul, stanza 3.

literally in the middle of nowhere, under the open skies streaming seamlessly into vast prairies, there were moments of screaming out to the One burning in my heart with His purifying light. His answer often came through the written hand of St. John of the Cross, helping me to appreciate the peace of Christ being given in the midst of this constant battle against evil. For although the hermit is indeed on the front line of this spiritual battle, it is not so much as to face off with Satan, as to release the incredible graces Christ longs to send the world through a soul striving to abide in Him.

Many people might wonder why anyone would want to live as a hermit. It was a question asked by the two parishes where I was serving as pastor when they learned I was leaving them. They knew I had been a very active diocesan priest for the past nine years. In trying to provide an answer, I came to appreciate the wisdom of St. Bruno, the founder of the Carthusians, who explained that "only the love of God explains and really justifies dedicating oneself to the contemplative life."[11]

It may be hard for some to accept that "the hermit is not called to govern, or to preach or to do good works."[12] "People in the world think it trifling"[13] to consecrate one's life "to pray, to suffer for his fellow men and to make sure that the office of prayer and praise is performed on their behalf."[14] "They have never tried its weight!"[15] For "this is no slight matter, no easy goal."[16] The hermit perseveres in this hidden mystery because they have reached the

[11] André Ravier, S.J., *Saint Bruno the Carthusian* (San Francisco: Ignatius Press, 1995), 142–143.

[12] A Monk, *The Hermitage Within*, trans. Alan Neame (London: Darton, Longman and Todd, 1999), 127.

[13] Ibid., 81–82.

[14] Ibid., 127.

[15] Ibid., 82.

[16] William of St. Thierry, *The Golden Epistle*, trans. Theodore Berkeley, O.C.S.O. (Kalamazoo, MI: Cistercian, 1980), 14.

conviction expressed by Pope Pius XI that "those whose assiduous zeal is devoted to prayer and penance make a greater contribution to the progress of the Church and to the salvation of mankind than do the laborers employed in cultivating the Lord's field; for if they were not to call down the abundance of divine graces to water that field, the laborers of the gospel would derive a much poorer harvest from their toils.... If in past ages, the Church had to rely on her anchorites, we need more than ever today that should exist and prosper."[17]

As a fruit of this vocation as a hermit, I would give a few eight-day retreats each year to the Missionaries of Charity and would teach in our permanent diaconate formation program. Throughout those years in the hermitage, the material on *The Dark Night* was taught every year in this program and presented in more than twenty retreats throughout the world for the Missionaries of Charity. It was a blessing to see so many souls recognize in themselves this path of contemplation as marked off by St. John of the Cross. We were surprised to learn that the "nodding off" we were embarrassed to admit happening during our regularly committed time of prayer might be what St. John describes as the Lord's way of leading a soul to contemplation. The questions and honest concerns raised while presenting this material enabled God to mold and shape it.

While living as a hermit, I adhered to the wise advice that "you must be content to lose yourself entirely ... to influence others directly even by the pen, is not one of the pursuits envisaged for the desert."[18] In the mystery of God's will, mostly due to health conditions, I returned in 2013 to being a very active diocesan priest. The "notes" that were often requested on the retreat material, you are

[17] Pope Pius XI, Apostolic Constitution *Umbratilem* (July 8, 1924), as found in *The Hermitage Within*, 129.

[18] *The Hermitage Within*, 10.

now holding in your hands as the book *And You Will Find Rest: What God Does in Prayer.*

As mentioned earlier, proper timing and experience of life do play a large factor in appreciating the writings of St. John of the Cross. In the various presentations on this material, it became evident that a few other challenges need to be addressed for the modern-day reader. Before reading St. John, we need to understand the terms on which he will build. We need to know what is the *lower part of the soul* and the *higher part of the soul,* the *senses* and the *spirit,* the *active purifications* and the *passive purifications.*

Then, the very specific understanding St. John has of contemplation, describing it as "the dark night,"[19] needs to rise above the vast and varied ways we have heard contemplation previously described.

Finally, the effort to go chapter by chapter through *The Dark Night* can prove to be so stark that at times people would openly ask me to remind them why anyone in their right mind would want to be subjected to it.

It is true, St. John of the Cross is stark and systematic in his effort to spell out the *path of purification.* His good friend, St. Teresa of Ávila, is anything but stark and systematic. Scattered and savoring might be a better description. Although she is no stranger to the path of purification, her writing of *The Interior Castle* is an effort to help us appreciate "the precious things that can be found in the soul."[20] It eventually struck me how she could help us along this dark *path of purification* with her colorful insights on the *pure experiences of God.*

It is not too far a stretch to suggest that their contact with one another may have had some influence on their writing of *The Dark Night* and *The Interior Castle.* St. Teresa was made prioress of the

[19] St. John of the Cross, *The Dark Night,* 1.8.1.

[20] St. Teresa of Ávila, *The Interior Castle,* 1.1.2.

Convent of the Incarnation in Ávila in the year 1571. She appointed St. John as the spiritual director and confessor for her and the other 130 nuns who lived there. It appears he remained there from 1572 to 1577. St. Teresa wrote *The Interior Castle* in 1577. St. John wrote the poem "The Dark Night" sometime between 1577 and 1579, and then the explanation between 1584 and 1585.

Regardless of the influence they may have had on one another in composing those texts, it has been my experience, through the many presentations on this material, that their texts of *The Dark Night* and *The Interior Castle* beautifully accompany us together on the path to contemplation.

After explaining the terms on which St. John will build, and providing an understanding of contemplation as he would understand it, we will go chapter-by-chapter through the first four dwellings of *The Interior Castle,* then on to "The Dark Night of the Senses," and finally to the fifth dwelling of the *The Interior Castle.* This has proven to provide a powerful context for many souls to appreciate the path of contemplation as it unfolds in our soul. Be warned that this, too, is not a one-time read; you will not be able to simply breeze through it. It is my hope that you will find in it wisdom to carry with you as you strive to consent in prayer to "take my yoke upon you and learn from me" (Matt. 11:29) and find the "rest" only God can lead you into.

You will, of course, appreciate that this is not the complete journey with *The Dark Night* and *The Interior Castle.* Perhaps one day the second part, combining the sixth and seventh dwelling of *The Interior Castle* with "The Dark Night of the Spirit," will also be in your hands.

Part 1

Active Purifications of Our Senses and Spirit

Chapter 1

To See God As He Really Is

(1 John 3:2)

When we hear St. Teresa speak of the supernatural, of "what the Lord does in the soul," our attention is easily diverted by what we know of people who have seen visions, heard voices, or witnessed miracles. Learning of such events can leave us hoping for something similar to occur in our lives and even wondering why it doesn't. Why doesn't God speak to me in the same way He spoke to them?

The short answer, provided by St. Teresa and St. John, is that this doesn't necessarily lead us into *His rest.* In fact, they actually advise us to avoid such communications as they often leave us restless and can distract us from the true purpose of prayer.

St. Teresa and St. John will help us appreciate that there are two levels by which Our Lord communicates to the human soul: through the *senses* and through the *faculties of our soul.* When God chooses to communicate by way of a voice or a vision, it requires Him to take on a form that our human senses can appreciate. It is telling that when our Blessed Mother appeared at Lourdes, she looked like a young French woman, while her apparition in Guadalupe is very much of a pregnant Mexican woman. Our Lord's appearance to St. Faustina has Him looking rather Polish. Every voice seems to be heard in one's native tongue.

God is a pure spirit, and the way He ordinarily communicates is beyond what "eye can see and ear can hear" (see 1 Cor. 2:9). For God to speak to us now, as He desires to speak with us for all eternity, we must be willing to go beyond the senses. Be assured that this is not a complicated method of prayer; it is, in fact, a much simpler process than hoping for a voice, vision or miracle. It is what I like to refer to as *the ordinary path to holiness.*

The term *ordinary* in no way implies that it is inferior to the *extraordinary*. The Church refers to the priest or deacon as the *ordinary* minister of Communion. Receiving Holy Communion through them is the preferred method. There are, however, occasions when the *ordinary* path of receiving Communion is supplemented with the use of *extraordinary* ministers of Communion.

The *ordinary path* by which Our Lord desires to speak to the soul of every human being is the preferred method. If our hearts are set on something *extraordinary,* it will be difficult for us to be led by Our Lord into His rest. It is not unlike the story of Naaman the leper who was instructed by the prophet Elisha to wash seven times in the Jordan River to be cured. It sounded a little too *ordinary* to bear the miraculous fruit Namaan was looking for. He was at first reluctant to even respond. His servants persuaded him to not disregard this seemingly meaningless activity. They counseled Namaan, "If the prophet had told you to do something extraordinary, would you not have done it? All the more now ... should you do as he said" (2 Kings 5:13).

If the path to enter into His rest were marked off by an *extraordinary* method of prayers and penances, we would all likely be scampering over one another to do exactly what was laid out, step-by-step. Well, since the *ordinary path* is a much simpler one, to "be still and know that I am God" (Ps. 46:11), "all the more should we do as they have said."

To *be still* requires a committed effort to place our trust in the *ordinary* way God desires to lead our soul into His rest. Just as Namaan remained restless in his desire for something *extraordinary,* if we are waiting for God to speak to us through a voice, vision, or miracle, it will prove difficult to *be still* when He comes to prepare our hearts to see Him "as he really is" (1 John 3:2). The blessings of truly knowing God and seeing Him "as he really is" are gifts reserved to the pure of heart: "Blessed are the pure of heart, for they shall see God" (Matt. 5:8). *The ordinary path to holiness* is well marked by this Beatitude.

The organ with which we see God best is not our eye; it is our heart. For the heart to see anything worth noting, the heart must be pure. Purity of heart requires an ongoing two-part process of purification. The first part is our own efforts to be pure. The second is the activity of God, which is able to purify us at a level we alone are not capable of doing. Without this activity of God, our heart could never hope to be led to the purity necessary to see Him.

The activity of God that is needed to purify our heart is what St. John of the Cross is intent upon helping us navigate. During a retreat offered in 2006 to the Missionaries of Charity in Memphis, Tennessee, on his material of *The Dark Night,* it became evident that something was needed to help them appreciate the terms with which he was guiding us. In between sessions I began praying for some type of tool to help them to see the difference between the *lower part of the soul* and the *higher part of the soul,* the *senses* and the *spirit,* the *active purifications* and the *passive purifications.* It was there that the *Diagram of Creation,* found on the following page, was first inspired. As the saying goes a picture is worth a thousand words, the *Diagram of Creation* is a tool that can help us to better visualize the glorious plan God has for us to be led into His rest.

Jesus beautifully expressed this plan in His prayer for us to "be one, as you, Father, are in me and I in you, that they also may be in us.... that the love with which you loved me may be in them and I in them" (John 17:21, 26). May the following diagram serve to enhance our appreciation for how all of creation is designed to work together for the very purpose of allowing Our Lord to lead us to where we will *find rest* for our souls.

The large outer triangle represents the Holy Trinity: Father, Son, and Holy Spirit. Outside of this triangle, nothing exists. Within this triangle lies all of God's glorious creation.

The circle within the Holy Trinity represents the world, composed of the four classical elements: fire, wind, land, and water. You will notice gaps in between these elements; they are there for a

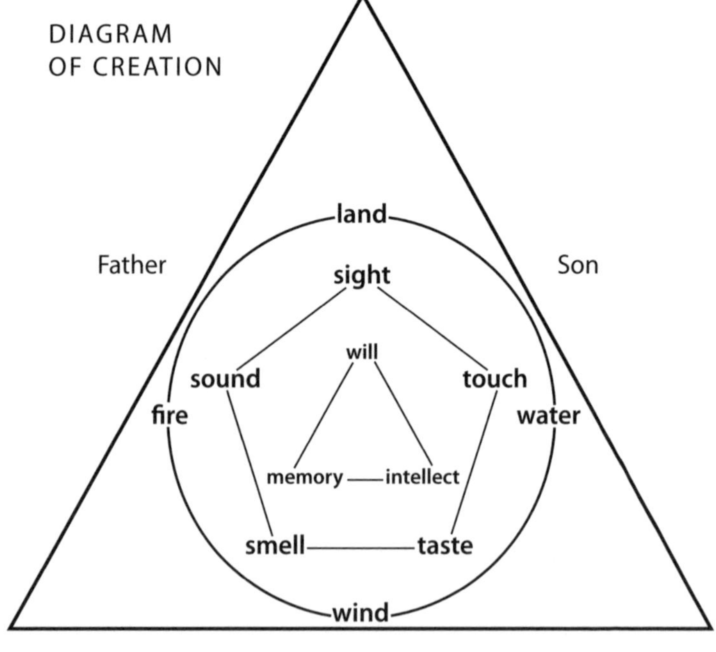

purpose. They illustrate how God communicates to us, how His glory breathes through these gates of His creation. Think for a moment of how evident His presence is in a beautiful landscape, a refreshing breeze after a rainfall, or the healing warmth of the sun's rays. I find God's presence powerfully communicated on the beach — the land, the sea, the wind, and the fire of the sun — all simultaneously breathing of His glorious presence.

Within this circle is a pentagon, which is meant to resemble the shape of a house. In his poem, "The Dark Night," St. John of the Cross refers to his senses as a house: "My house now being all stilled." So, this five-sided house is meant to illustrate the five human senses: sight, sound, smell, touch, and taste. The gaps are again there for a purpose: they represent the doors to one's house through which God longs to enter and bring His restful presence. Reflect for a moment on the beauty of these doors: the sight of a good friend, the sound of a laughing child, a running brook, the smell of a flower, the touch of a loved one, and the taste of your favorite meal. All are beautiful opportunities to experience the presence of God.

It is worth mentioning here the so-called "smells and bells" of the Catholic Church. The bells draw our attention to God, and the smell of incense makes us aware that we are in our Father's house.

Within this pentagon is another triangle. This interior triangle represents the soul, where the Holy Trinity desires to make His dwelling. The God of all creation, outside of which nothing can exist, has chosen to make His dwelling within our very soul.

The triangle also reminds us of a castle, and St. Teresa of Ávila refers to the soul as the *interior castle.* This *interior castle* — the soul — is composed of three faculties: the *intellect,* the *memory,* and the *will.* These are the *faculties of our soul* through which we are led to a more intimate experience of God's presence. As for the gaps, let us refer to them as the windows of our soul through which God longs to shine His light. How brilliantly His light of revelation shines through the window of our intellect with faith, giving substance in our memory to hope in what has been revealed, moving the will to respond to the revelation of His love with our love.

Within this inner triangle lies the human heart — not the physical beating heart, but as the *Catechism of the Catholic Church* spells out: "The heart is the dwelling-place where I am, where I live.... The heart is our hidden center, beyond the grasp of our reason and of others; only the Spirit of God can fathom the human heart and know it fully.... It is the place of truth, where we choose life or death. It is the place of encounter ... it is the place of covenant."[21] It is here that God may be in us, and we in Him. It is here that we are able to enter into His rest.

This diagram helps us appreciate how God radiates through all of creation with the clear aim to illuminate our human heart. In prayer, many experience His light as being filtered through the gates of this world's elements to enter the doors of our senses and finally to shine through the windows of our soul into our thirsting heart.

To the pure of heart, however, there is a path by which He passes through no doors and shines through no windows. It is a path known only to Our Lord, a path referred to as *infused prayer*. St. Teresa describes how "He wants to enter the center of the soul without going through any door, as He entered the place where His disciples were (after the resurrection) when He said, *'pax vobis'* (peace be with you)" (John 20:19).[22]

We cannot make such a delightful communication happen by our own efforts alone. This can only be accomplished by the activity of God.

We can, however, begin to dispose ourselves to be more ready to be led by Him when He chooses to show us the way. If the doors of

[21] CCC 2563.

[22] St. Teresa of Ávila, *The Interior Castle*, 5.1.12.

our senses are blocked and the windows of our soul covered with filth, we will be doing ourselves no favors when trying to respond to His invitation to "follow me."

So there needs to be a process of preparing our hearts, a way of purification, through which our heart is more ready to open when Our Lord knocks and can be illuminated when His Light begins to shine upon us. This process of opening the doors of our senses and washing the windows of our soul needs to be performed by both oneself and by God.

Active Purifications

The *active purifications* are our efforts to purify our heart by removing the things that block the doors of our senses and mar the windows of our soul. Our best efforts at self-denial are not able to bring about the purity of heart needed to see God. However, they are necessary to prepare us for when His hand eventually comes to lead us. We cannot be led into His rest without first making the effort to enter into His yoke.

Passive Purifications

The *passive purifications* are the times when the hand of God comes to open our doors and wash our windows. It is passive, because it is by the hand of God that we are now being purified. It is not entirely passive, however; we still need to give our consent.

The active purifications and the passive purifications happen at both the level of our senses and the faculties of our soul.

There are four classical levels of purification:

- ✠ Active purification of senses
- ✠ Active purification of the faculties of the soul
- ✠ Passive purification of senses
- ✠ Passive purification of the faculties of the soul.

These four levels of purification comprise the *ordinary path* by which Our Lord can lead us into the rest of a pure heart that sees God.

If you are feeling a bit confused at this point, do not be alarmed; the purpose of this book is to take us step-by-step through this process of purification.

Part 1 examines the *active purifications* of our *senses* and *spirit.*

Part 2 familiarizes us with the *passive purification* of the *senses.*

Part 3 helps us appreciate the *passive purification* of the *spirit.* (This will be addressed in a future volume.)

Why Is My Heart Not Pure?

If God wants to communicate so beautifully to us, why didn't He just create us that way? The answer: He did. The often-forgotten subject of Original Sin is what led us away from the rest God created us to enjoy in Him. The whole work of Creation was intended to lead us into His rest. "On the seventh day God completed the work he had been doing; he rested.... God blessed the seventh day and made it holy, because on it he rested from all the work he had done in creation" (Gen. 2:2–3).

In the beginning, there was beautiful harmony between the *senses* and the *faculties of the soul* as they worked together in our purpose of remaining in the rest of God.

So what happened? There was a freedom that remained to test us in this harmony. There was that tree in the middle of the garden (Gen. 3:3), "pleasing to the eye and enticing for the wisdom that it could give" (v. 6). The one thing God told us not to do, as a way of ensuring that our choice to follow Him was free, just could not escape our curiosity. Our hearts became restless, as they refused to rest in God.[23]

[23] See St. Augustine, "Our hearts are restless until they rest in You." *Confessions,* trans. Henry Chadwick (Oxford: Oxford University Press, 1991), bk. 1, par. 1., p. 3.

The *Catechism* explains that although Original Sin is erased by Baptism, its effects on our human nature remain, which weaken us and leave us inclined to evil.[24] Original Sin does not totally corrupt our human nature; it wounds the natural powers proper to it, making us subject to ignorance, suffering, and death, and inclined to sin.[25]

Our natural inclination to rest in God has been wounded and weakened. Original Sin is more of a reality than we might ever come to appreciate.

Before we embark upon the path of purification that will lead us back into His rest, it is helpful to recall the beauty of God's intention in creating us as we are.

The Goodness Of God's Creation

"I praise you Lord, for I am wonderfully made" (Ps. 139:14).

The day when the first human was formed out of dust, "God looked at everything he had made, and he found it very good" (Gen. 1:31). We have been created very good! We have been made in the very image of God.[26] It is His breath breathing through the dust of our body that gives us life. The life of God is breathing through us. Every fiber of our being was made to be alive for the glory of God. We have been "wonderfully made."

The Senses

St. John of the Cross refers to the senses as the *lower part* of our soul. They are the primary level at which we experience God communing with us. Each of our senses was given to help lead our soul into His rest.

[24] CCC 405.

[25] Ibid.

[26] "God created man in the image of himself." (Gen. 1:27).

Sight

Our sense of sight was given to behold the goodness of God's creation, to help us see creation as God sees it. Our sense of sight enables us to look beyond mere appearances and behold that *it is good* for the simple reason that God created it.

God never stops looking at us and saying that we are good. Sometimes we aren't doing good things, but that doesn't trump the goodness of who we are. This is the very reason why Jesus came to save us. He was able to see beyond our sinful appearance and behold our goodness.

Imagine the rest we might experience if we truly saw others as God sees them. Our human tendency is to determine the goodness of God's creation on the basis of who and what is good *for me.* The result of eating from the tree of the knowledge of good and evil is real. It was from there that our sense of sight led us into the restlessness of establishing our own criteria for who and what is good or evil. We now look at people and things and determine their goodness on the basis of whether or not they are good *for me.*

The saints are great models in helping us recover our sense of sight. St. Francis of Assisi was restless around lepers; the mere sight of them would revolt him. In his desire to see them as God sees them, he went up to a leper and kissed him. That was one of St. Francis's first steps to enter into the rest of God, which enabled him to become a great instrument of peace. St. Teresa of Calcutta began her mission of peace by going up to the most decrepit person and treating him with compassion. When he asked why she was doing this, her reply was "Because I love you." Mother Teresa's clear sight continues to serve to open the eyes of those tempted to restlessly look away from the destitute and fail to recognize Jesus' presence in what she would call the "distressing disguise of the poorest of the poor."

In seeing creation as God sees creation, we enter into His rest.

Sound

Our sense of hearing was given so we could listen to God and obey Him. The Latin word for "listen" is *audire,* and "to obey" is *obaudire.* To obey communicates that I have heard what was being spoken to me. There was a mother who commented on how she would tell her children to do their homework, pick up their room, take out the garbage, and so forth. An hour later, she would see them still lounging on the couch watching television. So, she would remind them again, "Do your homework, pick up your room, and take out the garbage." To which they would respond, "We heard you, Mom." Then came this telling reprimand, "I know you *heard* me. *Obey* me!"

If we choose to obey only what is pleasing to our ears, we will never be led to a place of true rest. Our restless society has an unprecedented capacity for listening only to what we want to hear. Music streaming services enable people to only listen to the songs they like to hear. Caller ID enables us to answer only the people we want to listen to. We go church shopping until we hear someone whom we don't have to obey because they are merely "tickling our ears."

Society has become increasingly deaf in its ability to listen to God. God's "still small voice" (1 Kings 19:12) speaks best in silence, and there isn't much silence out there. Even in prayer, it often seems more a monologue than a dialogue. How can we be led into His rest if we don't remain still enough to hear and obey His invitation to enter into His yoke?

Touch

Our sense of touch is the crowning of our human senses. There are other beings in God's creation that are superior to us in the other senses: they can smell, hear, see, and taste better than us. Our human sense of touch stands alone in the awareness it brings of how to give most fully of ourselves.

The heart of Christ was so pure that He could not touch without giving. In the midst of a large crowd pressing upon Him, the woman with a hemorrhage touched the hem of His garment. Christ could feel that "power had gone out through Him" and so asked, "Who touched me?" (Mark 5:30).

St. Teresa of Calcutta was a champion at the sense of touch. If she shook your hand, she put the other one on top of yours. When she met a baby, she covered it with caresses. It is through the sense of touch that we give most fully of ourselves. The beauty of the marital embrace is realized when the sense of touch is an act of giving oneself to the other.

It is with our great sense of touch that the temptation to be selfish can rear its ugly head. When our sense of touch is used to take rather than to give, true violence enters into the world. It is the difference between hugging and mugging. We enter into the rest of a hug by giving ourselves to another's embrace; we mug them by restlessly taking them by force into our arms.

God gave us the sense of touch to enter into the rest that comes when we give of our self.

Smell

Our sense of smell was given to awaken us to the presence of God.

The sense of smell is perhaps the quickest path to our human heart. Good smells are obvious: someone can tell us they are preparing our favorite meal, but the smell of their cooking gets our salivary glands working. In the liturgy, incense is used to awaken our senses to the presence of God. Both the Old and New Testament refer to prayer as arising before God as incense (Ps. 141:2). The book of Revelation describes "an angel standing before the face of God, thurible in hand.... The fragrant incense soaring aloft was the prayer of God's people on earth" (Rev. 8:3–4).

Smell is indeed a great source of pleasure, so enjoyable that we are tempted to use it for pleasure only. We tend to plug our nose at what is repugnant, perfume what we can, and try to "sniff out" danger. In spiritual terms we like the *odor of sanctity* but plug our nose at the *stench of sin*. Both are part of our human condition.

God did not plug His nose at the stench of our sin. In fact, it was precisely that smell that awakened Him to the need of having a sacrifice offered for us — the sacrifice of His Son on the Cross for the salvation of the world.

We would rather plug our noses at sacrifices. But the Old Testament teaches us that God loves the smell of a sacrifice. Think for a moment how the offering of an entire animal to be burned as a sacrifice is recounted over and over again as "a sweet smelling oblation to the LORD" (Lev. 1:9). Have you ever smelled the body of an entire animal being burned? It is far from sweet-smelling. Just think of the smell of burning hair alone, and that is just the beginning of a carcass that is going to be burned beyond a crisp. Who likes the smell of burnt food?

God loves the smell of a sacrifice that comes from the heart of a human striving to be at peace with God.

Sometimes those in need do not smell too pleasant, testifying to their need of assistance. When I was a seminarian in Rome, every Thursday I would help at San Gregorio, a shelter for the homeless provided through the Missionaries of Charity. Normally they would ask me to sort through dirty old clothes donated to them for other, poorer missions. One day they asked me to go upstairs to help a brother seminarian with a man in the bathroom. As I entered the second floor where the bathroom was, I smelled a stench that was truly repulsive. I thought maybe someone had vomited and hoped that it might already be in the process of being cleaned up. Looking around, there was no mess to be seen. As I walked toward the bathroom, the smell intensified. I could only imagine that I was being directed toward the source of that smell. When I opened the door to the bathroom, my suspicions were confirmed.

There in the room was my brother seminarian, already in the process of helping clean a man who had been literally decaying in the streets. This man was in a condition I had never before seen. He had lost his arms sheltering a child from the explosion of a grenade in the Balkans and was now living on the streets of Rome. It was clear that he would not be living on earth much longer. As I said, his body was in a condition I had never seen before. I won't go into the gory detail; suffice it to say that this was the first time I had seen worms living on human flesh. My senses were revolted. I was not looking beyond what I saw. The smell was not awakening me to the presence of God. My touch was not ready to give. In fact, I thought I was going to pass out.

The smell was so repugnant that I was continually gagging. My friend had already undressed this man and had him sitting in the bathtub. Seeing that only one person could touch him at a time, and to regain my senses, I volunteered to take his clothes out to the dump to alleviate the smell. It was a good idea, but with very selfish motives. I took my time completing this task, hoping that the majority of the touching might be done by the time I returned. On reaching the second floor and nearing that same bathroom, my senses began to revolt at the memory of what I had seen. Across the hall from the bathroom was a chapel. I quickly ducked in there for a moment to ask God for the strength to do what I alone could not. To my utter surprise, whom did I find in that chapel, but my friend who was supposed to be in the bathroom helping to clean up that poor man. I asked, "What are you doing in *here*?" He replied, "What are *you* doing in here?" Then the sister who had asked us to help this man entered the chapel to demand of us, "What are you *doing* in here?"

We explained that we had never encountered a human being in this condition and that we didn't think we could do it. She quickly responded, "Of course *you* cannot do it; you must allow *Christ* to do it. You must see Jesus in this man, and you must be Jesus for him." Our spiritual senses were quickly sobered up, and we went back in to help this saintly man who was waiting in the bathtub. We were now able to look beyond his appearance; the smell was now awakening us to God's presence, and our touch became a means to give this man what Christ longed to give him. Jesus was leading us into His rest.

When we finished helping this man in the bathroom, I will never forget his humble gratitude. I will also always remember the eagerness with which some sisters rushed toward him to continue helping him. One went immediately to his feet to address his wounds, while another shaved and disinfected his lice-ridden hair. Their senses were much purer than mine. I learned a lot from the experience of that day, and I continue to learn from it.

Taste

Finally, consider the sense of taste: taste is really a wonderful sense; it helps us appreciate the goodness of God in how He created us. Taste is given as an accompanying pleasure for doing a necessary good. We all need to eat in order to survive. God made eating such a pleasant experience that we are tempted to eat just for pleasure. We become indulgent. Instead of enjoying the restful pleasure that accompanies the nourishment of our bodies, we eat just to savor the taste, even to our body's detriment.

Sleep is another necessary good that is accompanied by a truly restful pleasure. Here too we can become indulgent. We can stay in bed beyond what is necessary for our rejuvenation, for the mere pleasure of it, which actually ends up making us all the more tired.

The proper use of taste also applies to necessary spiritual works. It is necessary for us to pray and do spiritual and corporeal works of mercy. I have yet to see someone returning from time spent in such spiritual activities without an interior sense of pleasure. Many times people will debate whether they should go to church on Sunday, yet when they go, it would be rare to hear them say it was a bad idea. You may need to convince a group of adolescents to help rake the lawn of an elderly couple, but watch them when they return. They all feel good about themselves. Spiritual activities taste good. But here too lies the danger of becoming a spiritual glutton. This happens when we engage in spiritual activities merely for our personal pleasure rather than for the love of God. As we will later learn, spiritual gluttony leads us away from entering into the rest of God.

I hope this review of the senses renews in us the awareness of how we have been "wonderfully made." The process of purification is in no way intended to make our life less enjoyable, as some are tempted to regard such spiritual exercises. The process of purification is meant to restore us to the fullness of life. Christ proclaimed, "I came that they may have life, and have it to the full" (John 10:10). Without the purification Christ came to bring us, our quest for fulfillment would remain restless.

The Fall of Our Senses

God promised Adam and Eve that the moment they decided to eat from the tree of knowledge of good and evil, they would be doomed to die (Gen. 2:17). Although they did not physically die at that exact moment, the death they incurred that day was much more severe. Had it only been a physical death, their souls might have remained with God. From the moment of the Fall, Adam, Eve, and all of their children were banned from the Garden of Eden (Gen. 3:23). A brief look at the account of the Fall might help us appreciate that it was the fall of every one of our senses.

Sight: "The woman saw that the tree was good for food, pleasing to the eyes, and desirable for gaining wisdom" (Gen. 3:6).

This was the first time the sense of sight was used to look at something and failed to see what God sees. Eve looked at this tree, knowing that God had commanded her not to even touch it. There was no need for her to search for ways to "become like gods" (Gen. 3:5); it was already well within God's plan for us to "be like him" (1 John 3:2). Instead of resting in obedience to the command of God, she became restless in thinking that God might be keeping her from something she would enjoy. This is the error behind every choice to disobey God: the thought that He is not a generous God, that we cannot trust Him, not entirely.

The disastrous effect of eating from the tree of the knowledge of good and evil is real. God knew how restless that knowledge would make us. As children of Eve, we are ingrained to use our sense of sight to look at creation and determine for ourselves what is good and what is evil.

Touch: "She took some of its fruit" (Gen. 3:6).

In the Fall, Eve used her sense of touch not to give, but to take. God was not giving her this fruit. Eve was taking it. We have since strayed far beyond taking. Grabbing better describes the current human condition. How blind we can be not to acknowledge God as the giver of our daily bread. We take way more than we need, grabbing and hoarding at the expense of depriving others of basic necessities.

I experienced a small taste of what God might feel about such hoarding. In the spring, I put out some thistle seed for the finches to eat. It is free food. If you could see how they fight over it — they tend to behave as if it is all theirs. Even the birds of the field can forget that it is all a gift from God. Jesus knew of this wound. When He sent out His disciples, He was careful to teach them to remember that all they have is a gift from God: "Freely have you received, freely shall you give" (Matt. 10:8).

Taste: "and ate it" (Gen. 3:6).

God had given Adam and Eve the freedom to eat from any tree in the garden except this one. This was not eating for nourishment but for the sheer pleasure of tasting what was forbidden. How easy it is to be controlled by our desires. This is symbolized in the habit of going shopping just for the sake of looking. Our necessities are all met. We just want to tantalize our taste buds.

Sound: "When they heard the sound of the LORD God moving about in the garden at the breezy time of day, the man and his wife hid themselves from the LORD God among the trees" (Gen. 3:8).

The sound of God would have normally been a source of great joy for Adam and Eve. How eagerly they would have gone out to meet Him! However, they had not obeyed what God had commanded. Their disobedience made them anxious instead of eager to hear the sound of God. They had blocked the door to what would have normally been a beautiful opportunity to commune with God.

It might be worth asking what our reaction would be to the sound of God entering our garden at any given moment of the day. Is the door to our house open for Him to enter? Or is there something that would cause us to want to hide?

Smell: There is no Scripture passage to quote here, but there could have been one about the sacrifice God was inviting Adam to offer that day.

Adam was right beside his wife in their honeymoon bliss when the serpent came to tempt her to do the one thing God told them not to do. Adam should have stepped in to defend his wife from this attack of the evil one. Then there would have been a sacrifice to smell. Adam sniffed out that sacrifice and didn't make it.

That was why a "last Adam" (1 Cor. 15:45) was needed, who would offer Himself as a sacrifice for the sake of His Bride, the Church. There has been no sweeter smell, whose pervasive aroma still gives us hope.

As the "book of life" (Rev. 20:12) continues to be written with our every deed, what passages are being omitted due to our fear of offering our lives as a "living sacrifice" (Rom. 12:1)?

The third chapter of the book of Genesis has given us an account of the first rebellion of the senses. This history continues to be written out in our own bodies. As the *Catechism* taught us earlier, we are wounded and weakened: inclined to evil, making us subject to ignorance, suffering, death and inclined to sin.[27]

Our senses were not alone in this rebellion. Had the faculties of our soul remained true to God, nothing of lasting consequence would have happened that day in Eden. There is a deeper level of communication beyond our senses. It is there that God informs our intellect of the plan He has for our life, where our memory holds the hope of this plan, and where our will is placed in the battle for whether or not we freely choose this plan of faith.

Let us now turn our attention to what St. John of the Cross would recognize as the "higher part of our soul." What do these faculties of the soul precisely mean?

Faculties of the Soul: Intellect, Memory, and Will

We live in an age where so much attention is given to the body that it might seem as if the body were eternal. It is not. Each of our bodies

[27] *CCC* 405.

will return to dust, and a new body will be given to us at the final resurrection. The soul we die with, however, will be ours forever.

St. Thérèse of Lisieux was memorably taught by her sister, Pauline, that in Heaven everyone's soul will be filled to the brim with the glory of God.[28] Pauline had St. Thérèse take a tiny sewing thimble and their father's large drinking tumbler and fill them both to the brim with water. This helped Thérèse to recognize how "in heaven God will grant His Elect as much glory as they can take."[29] The point is that our time on earth will determine the capacity of our soul. In Heaven, each soul will be filled to capacity with the love of God. Now is the time that we determine whether our capacity to receive God's love will be that of a tiny sewing thimble or of a big drinking tumbler. In terms of the "new wine" that Jesus says He will drink with us in "the kingdom of my Father" (Matt. 26:29), some will have the capacity of a small shot glass; others will be more of a big Bavarian beer mug.

Here on earth our body has a huge influence on the soul, so much that the senses are referred to as the "lower part of our soul." The body and the soul are described as the matter and form of a human being. The body is the matter, the physical material with which we are made. The soul is what gives form to who we truly are. A good example of this distinction is found in a balloon. The rubber is the matter and the air blown in gives it form. A balloon can also be filled with water, giving it a much different form. What we fill the matter of the balloon with will determine whether the balloon rises up toward the heavens or comes crashing down to earth with a splash.

Similarly, both the senses of our body and the faculties of our soul work together to determine whether our soul rises as a vessel of grace or comes crashing down as an instrument of destruction.

[28] St. Thérèse of Lisieux, *Story of a Soul*, 3rd ed., trans. John Clarke, O.C.D. (Washington, D.C.: ICS, 1996), 45.

[29] Ibid.

The senses, as the "lower part of the soul," lead us at a more primary level to enter into God's rest. The faculties, as the "higher part of the soul," open the path to enter into the depths of this rest. Here they are in detail:

Intellect

The intellect is given for us to consider the true path that will lead to our rest. It is different than the thinking that goes on in our imagination, which often has little to do with truth. There are different types of truth for our intellect to consider. There are historical truths, philosophical truths, and scientific truths. There are also the truths of our salvation. These are the truths revealed by God for the sake of leading us into His rest. The intellect is given to help us consider the path marked off for us by God, most especially through Jesus Christ.

Our intellect can be directly informed by God through prayer and indirectly through what we choose to fill it with. The books we read, the conversations we engage in, the television programs we watch, and so on, all serve to inform our intellect. We are free to choose whether our intellect will be filled with the wisdom of the gospel or with the ways of the world.

Our temptation is to think in a worldly way, rather than through the wisdom of the gospel. For example, Jesus teaches that "when someone strikes you on (your) right cheek, turn the other one to him as well" (Matt. 5:39). That wisdom is weighed against the historical truth that if I do turn the other cheek, it too is likely to get hit. The intellect is given for us to consider which truth we will live by.

Memory

The faculty of memory is given to record what truly happens. If you will excuse the pun, the memory is an often-forgotten faculty of the soul. It is a very powerful part of the soul. Our celebration of the Eucharist is our memorial of what truly happened.

Memory was given to help us remain rooted in the truth. It is here that war is often waged. Pontius Pilate demanded of Christ, “What is truth?” (John 18:38) The Truth was standing right before him. But Pilate was considering other truths, like the possible riot of the Jews if he did not condemn this innocent man.

Memory is prone to making slight alterations to what truly happened. It sometimes forgets the good or evil of a particular situation. In the midst of our success, memory can lose sight of the fact that good people helped us along our way. There are also traumatic events, particularly forms of abuse, after which our memory needs to keep the evil of what happened hazy to enable us to move forward. Eventually, even those memories will need to be healed. We need to be firmly rooted in the truth of God’s love for us. He does not abandon the soul, even when the free will of another soul chooses to do evil against it.

Our memory is there to keep us rooted in the truth of God’s mercy and justice. It also helps us to remember that the Cross is not our enemy — it is the instrument of our salvation.

In the midst of everything we allow our intellect to be influenced by, memory is given to help us remain rooted in what we have learned of God’s revelation. The more we fill our intellect with His Word, the more certain it is that our memory will guide us into the hope of entering into His rest. If we choose to fill our intellect with what the world has to say, the more likely our memory will leave us “anxious and worried about many things” (Luke 10:41).

Will

The will is God’s incredible gift of love to us humans, which enables us to freely choose what truth we will live by. We normally consider the choices we make truly best for us at the moment. It is here that we can be deceived.

It might seem that God would have been wiser to not grant such freedom of will, knowing how horribly it would be misused. However, not to give us this freedom would go against God's nature of love. Love does not coerce or manipulate. If God were to stop me just before I carried out any evil, I might eventually resent Him. If every time I was about to say a bad word, God reached out and grabbed my tongue, or if I were about to strike you on the cheek and God put His hand out to stop me, I would likely feel manipulated by God to do good.

The true glory of God lies in our free choices to know, love, and serve Him. The mystics have come to recognize the path of contemplation as the greatest act of charity. It is here that we freely consent to God's desire to purify our heart for a love that is able to see Him "as he really is" (1 John 3:2).

The word *virtue* describes a person choosing what is truly best. To do that, we need the freedom of will to choose for ourselves what truth we will live in.

Those, in a nutshell, are the faculties of the soul.

Here is how the Fall impacted every one of them.

The Fall of Our Faculties

Intellect: "The woman saw that the tree was … desirable for gaining wisdom" (Gen 3:6).

God had already informed the intellect of Adam and Eve of the necessity of staying away from this one tree, but the information they were receiving from other sources became all too enticing. What kind of wisdom was the woman seeking? It certainly was not the wisdom of God. It was the cruel temptation to try to "become like gods who know what is good and what is evil" (Gen. 3:5). We children of Eve often act like gods with a wisdom of this world that becomes impatient with God. Pope Benedict XVI observed in his inaugural homily how we often wish God would "show himself stronger, that he would strike decisively, defeating evil and creating a better world."[30] This is the wisdom of the world used by all the ideologies of power to "justify the destruction of whatever would stand in the way of progress and the liberation of humanity."[31] To freely choose to follow the path of faith "we suffer on account of God's patience. And yet, we need his patience.... The world is redeemed by the patience of God. It is destroyed by the impatience of man."[32]

God knew how restless the "knowledge of good and evil" would make us. That is why Jesus tried to steer us back onto the patient path of faith, teaching us to live "by every word that comes forth from the mouth of God" (Matt. 4:4).

Memory: (The serpent speaking:) "Did God really tell you not to eat from any of the trees in the garden?" "You will certainly not die!" (Gen. 3:1, 4)

Here, Eve's memory was being tested. Eve remembered correctly at first — there was only one tree God told them not to eat from. Her memory started to quickly fade in light of the temptation of new knowledge being placed before her. A slight alteration occurred in her memory about what type of death would commence for her by breaking this one command of God. The battle for her will was now on.

Will: "She took some of the fruit and ate it, and she gave some to her husband" (Gen. 3:6).

[30] Benedict XVI, Mass of Inauguration Homily (April 24, 2005).

[31] Ibid.

[32] Ibid.

Once her will chose to act against God's will, this became a watershed moment. She reached out to touch, not with the intention to give, but to take some of the fruit. God wasn't giving her this fruit; Eve was reaching out against His will to take it. She ate that fruit, not for nourishment, but for the taste of worldly wisdom. Then, since misery loves company, she took some more fruit for her husband.

This helps us appreciate the mess going on within us. As complex as the senses are, the faculties are even more intricately woven. Our intellect, memory, and will were created to support each other in freely choosing the path of God's will. Eve's memory should have kept answering this temptation with the truth that God doesn't tell lies. The death He promised would come. With Eve's slight alteration of the truth, we see how this initial rebellion has led to an ongoing war. But it is not a hopeless battle. For Adam and Eve's son Cain, who murdered his brother Abel, God recognized that "sin is a demon lurking at the door . . . yet you can be his master" (Gen. 4:7). The good news is that we can master this rebellion and allow God to use our senses and faculties to lead us into His rest.

The Law and the Call

St. John of the Cross is clear on what serves to restore peace to the faculties of our soul. In book two of *The Dark Night,* he spells out how the theological virtues of faith, hope, and love will lead the intellect, memory, and will into God's rest. We will flesh that out in a moment.

St. John's clarity on the remedy for the faculties left me pondering what might serve as a good prescription for our senses. Since there are five senses, we need an article of faith that corresponds with the same number.

The five books of Genesis, Exodus, Leviticus, Numbers, and Deuteronomy are known to the Jews as the *torah,* or the Law.[33] With the assistance of the Law, we are provided with a two-tiered approach to establishing God's rule over the rebellion of our body's senses and soul's faculties. These two tiers are the Law and the Call.

The Law serves to bring order to our senses so that our faculties can better respond to the Call of Jesus to "follow me." The Law and the Call are intimately connected. Christ made it clear that He did not come to abolish the Law; He came to fulfill it (Matt. 5:17). A faithful disciple of Christ will acknowledge how the Call to follow Jesus entails a resolve to lovingly fulfill all that the Law demands. We might easily recognize in our own spiritual journey the graduated response of moving from an observer of the Law to one who willingly decides to embrace the Call to "deny yourself, pick up your cross and follow me" (Luke 9:23).

The Law: Bringing Order to Our Senses

The Law serves to bring order to our senses. Our feet need to be pointed in the right direction so that when our Lord comes with the Call we might be more ready to actually follow Him.

Genesis: Sight

With each act of Creation in the first chapter of Genesis, God beholds what He created, and every single time, "God saw that it was good"—(Gen. 1:4, 10, 12, 18, 21, 25, 31). If God were to count the reasons for the goodness of creation, there would be just one: "I made it." Adam and Eve's view of creation became disordered when they developed their own criteria for what was good.

[33] "Introduction to the Pentateuch," in *The New Jerusalem Bible* (Garden City, NY: Doubleday, 1985), 5.

Throughout the book of Genesis, God is guiding His Chosen People to look at creation in a way that restores their sight to behold the goodness of His providence. After the flood, God establishes His covenant with Noah through the sign of a rainbow (Gen. 9:13). He shows Abram a symbol of his numerous descendants through the stars of the sky (Gen. 15:5). Rebekah is given a foreshadowing of her family's destiny through the birth of Jacob, who came out of her womb grasping the heel of his twin Esau, the firstborn, and who as an adult usurped Esau's birthright as the eldest (Gen. 25:26). Jacob and Joseph were able to perceive in their dreams the activity of God unfolding in their lives (Gen. 28:12–13; 37:5).

St. Paul came to see very clearly that "all things work for good for those who love God" (Rom. 8:28). For those who love God, even our every cross can be seen as being used by God to accomplish good. All of creation exists to work together for the good of our soul. We simply need to see it as God does.

Exodus: Taste

In Exodus, God is refining the taste of the Israelites to what is proper for their nourishment. As slaves in Egypt, the Israelites lost their hunger for true heavenly nourishment. When God led them out into the desert to refine their sense of taste, they revolted. "Why did we not die at Yahweh's hand in Egypt, where we used to sit round the flesh pots and could eat to our heart's content?" (Exod. 16:3). So distorted was their taste that God needed to restrict their diet for forty years. Providing them with manna, God says, "I will now rain down bread from heaven.... to test them in this way" (Exod. 16:4). It took time for them to appreciate the sweet taste of what alone can truly satisfy.

Forty years: It seems a telling number, as it is often in midlife that one realizes how unfulfilling the things of this world truly are. As good as worldly pleasures might taste, they fail to nourish, leaving us restless. How easy it is to become enslaved as did the Israelites. May the book of Exodus continue to serve to set God's people free to "taste and see how good is the LORD" (Ps. 34:8).

Leviticus: Touch

The tribe of Levi was set aside by God as priests to serve the Israelites. The book of Leviticus is addressed to them. It is almost entirely based upon laws that keep them in a state of legal (or ritual) purity. A part of their purity was established through the use of touch. The Levites were not to touch what God marked as unclean (Lev. 5:2–3; 7:21; 11:8, 31). To touch what God had declared unclean would make them unclean. What God does give them to touch, through the ritual sin offering, serves to restore purity to all it touches: "Whatever touches its flesh shall become sacred" (Lev. 6:20).

In short, we are to touch only what God gives us to touch. It is always good to ask ourselves whether the things we reach out to touch are being given to us by God.

Numbers: Smell

In the book of Numbers, we hear these words of God: "Take care to bring me my offering, my sustenance in the form of food burnt as a smell pleasing to me, at the proper time" (Num. 28:2). Again, a burnt offering would have a repugnant odor; it was the sacrifice made in obedience to God that rendered it pleasing to Him.

God loves the smell of sacrifice. It is an odor with which we, too, must become better accustomed. When we start to smell the burn of an offering, let us strive to recall how it is our "humble, contrite heart" (Ps. 51:19) that will prove to be the only "acceptable sacrifice" (Phil. 4:18).

Deuteronomy: Sound

The sound of God should not frighten us. In hearing God's commands, we should love to obey Him, for "his commandments are not burdensome" (1 John 5:3). The clear focus of the book of Deuteronomy is to get us to listen to God and obey Him.

> "Listen to the laws and customs which I am teaching you today … add nothing to what I command you, and take nothing from it, but keep the commandments of Yahweh your God just as I lay them down for you" (Deut. 4:1–2).
>
> "Listen, Israel, to the laws and customs that I proclaim to you today" (Deut. 5:1).
>
> "Listen then, Israel, keep and observe what will make you prosperous and numerous" (Deut. 6:3).

Do we make time to listen to the Word of God? If we only listen on Sunday to His Word, can we really hope to hear what He is trying to tell us? A friend of mine once commented, "Show me something you do for only an hour a week and I will show you something you are not very good at." It is true. What serious musician would practice only one hour a week? Which athletic program would be that shortsighted? How anxious the upcoming performance or game would become if we only practiced one hour that week.

Are we prepared to hear the sound of God entering into our garden today? Would we go out to meet Him with joy, or is some disobedience keeping us hiding in fear?

Seeing how the Law can help restore some order to the senses, let us now turn our attention to the faculties of our soul to learn how they are best equipped to answer the Call.

The Call: Balm for the Soul

Jesus came to call sinners (Luke 5:32). It was for the sick that He came calling (Luke 5:31). Our Divine Physician longs to lead us into the healing only He can give us. At Baptism, we receive His gifts of faith, hope, and love. These theological virtues are able to heal us at the deepest level. They guide our faculties to be led into His rest. In Heaven, St. Paul reminds us, only faith, hope, and love will remain (1 Cor. 13:13). The measure of every true disciple of Christ lies in their earnest efforts to allow faith, hope, and love to guide every step in their intellect, memory, and will. Through these gifts Jesus manifests that He is "the way and the truth and the life" (John 14:6).

Intellect: Faith, the Way

Faith teaches our intellect to think, not as the world thinks, but as God thinks. As we are reminded in the book of Isaiah, "My thoughts are not your thoughts, nor are your ways my ways, says the Lord. As high as the heavens are above the earth, so high are my ways above your ways and my thoughts above your thoughts" (Isa. 55:8–9). We need the gift of faith to show us the way to walk in this world, in particular, the way Christ has marked off for us. Jesus is the Way (John 14:6). The path of faith He calls us to walk heals our intellect of the warped, worldly way of thinking. We were given the gift of faith in Baptism and must pray daily for it to increase; "I do believe, help my unbelief!" (Mark 9:24).

Memory: Hope, the Truth

Hope heals the memory. Hope shows us the truth that God never abandons our soul, even when the free will of another has chosen to do evil against us. God does not intervene to stop the free will of any person. If He did, no person would be free. This does not mean that God abandons the soul of the afflicted. In fact, it is often those most deeply wounded whom Our Lord leads to enter most deeply into His rest.

I am amazed at the number of deeply wounded souls who find their way to a religious vocation. I am convinced it is Our Father's tenderness that draws them. He strives to teach them the truth that they are His beloved children. They are called to live in His house, be dressed in His clothes and nourished with His food. Jesus Himself lives right next door in the chapel's tabernacle. With such signs of our Heavenly Father's love, they are sure to find their place in His family.

May we all be led to the healing truth that enables us to "see what love the Father has bestowed on us that we may be called the children of God" (1 John 3:1). This truth will serve to keep us safe in the hope that "we shall be like him, for we shall see him as he really is" (1 John 3:2.)

WILL: LOVE, THE LIFE

Upon my ten-year anniversary of ordination, I was privileged to make a pilgrimage to Jerusalem where His Beatitude Michel Sabbah, archbishop and Latin patriarch of Jerusalem, gave this sound advice: "You must not be like others; you must be like Christ. In order for others to live, you must die. If you do not die, others will not live."

Jesus brought life to the world in freely choosing "not to do my own will but the will of the one who sent me" (John 6:38). Jesus's example of love helps us look beyond our immediate selfish desires and allow love to guide our will on the path that leads to the "fullness of life." Love alone can heal our will and lead us to life. "For whoever wishes to save his life will lose it, but whoever loses his life for my sake and the sake of the gospel will save it" (Mark 8:35).

Winning the War Within

In the life of Christ, we witness how the faculties of our souls were originally intended to work together. Jesus's intellect was guided by faith in thinking only of His Father's will. His memory was filled with hope to walk in faith, even upon the way of the Cross. His love for our Heavenly Father strengthened His will to freely choose this path of salvation for the world.

In Baptism, we were given the keys with which such harmony can be restored in us. Baptism not only washed us of the stain of Original Sin, it began to address our weak and wounded souls with the ointments of faith, hope, and love. These theological virtues lead the faculties of our soul to live in harmony again. When the faculties are not being guided by faith, hope, and love, a war goes on inside.

The diagram on the next page can help us appreciate this:

> Faith, hope, and love integrate our intellect, memory, and will. These faculties are meant to work together in our earthly struggle. Without faith, hope, and love to guide us, we become disintegrated.

A story that illustrates this is that of St. Peter walking on the water. In this story we have a man whose senses were giving his faculties all kinds of reasons to be filled with anxiety. The sight of the storm around him informed his intellect that there was cause for fear. His memory likely recalled such events in which the outcome was not good. He and his companions caught sight of what they thought was a ghost, and his will decided to panic. New information was then given for his intellect to process. He was assured that it was Jesus on the water and not a ghost. Jesus confirmed Peter's request to come out onto the water toward Him. Peter then allowed his intellect to be guided by faith. His fearful memories were restored by his hope in Jesus. This gave Peter the strength of will to decide to do what is humanly impossible. His loving confidence in Jesus got Peter to step out of the boat and walk toward Our Lord on water.

The man, who had been filled with anxiety about his safety while still in the boat, was now at peace with getting out of the boat during a raging storm, but that harmony was not to last. Peter's intellect became distracted by what sources other than his faith were telling him. He started to look around at the storm. Maybe he looked at himself and thought, "I can't do this!" He might have looked back at the boat and seen the disbelief in the faces of his brothers. Whatever the case, he took his eyes of faith off Jesus, quickly lost his peace, and nearly lost his life. Our Lord

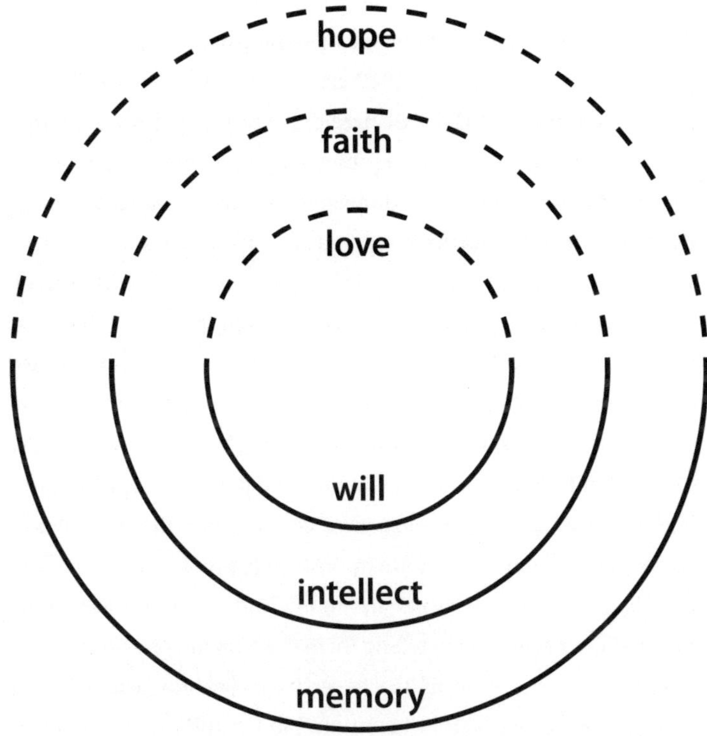

scolded Peter for his lack of faith — the faith that had held him as he walked on water.

There is an adage, "Fear knocks. Faith answers. No one is there." Had Peter kept answering his inner fears with faith, there would have been nothing behind that door that told him he was going to sink. This story can help us appreciate how Our Lord guides us into His rest through His gifts of faith, hope, and love. It illustrates well how the faculties are truly "the higher part of the soul." Peter's faith told his intellect to do things beyond what the senses would have said was possible. His faculties led him to rise above his senses and take that first step out onto the water. Peter had to deny his intellect what his senses were telling him. His faith became the substance of the hope that Jesus wouldn't let him sink. His love for Jesus led him to step out of the boat and walk on water.

I am moved to share the story of some Missionaries of Charity who were in Haiti during the 2010 earthquake. What they did in the aftermath was nothing short of heroic, if not miraculous. Had they been told a week earlier the things they might see, how ruggedly they would need to live, and what God would need to accomplish through their hands, they would have thought it impossible. Quite simply, when the time came, they were walking on water. After the earthquakes, the sisters had no form of outside communication. There was no electricity. Any building that remained standing could not be used out of fear of its instability. With only the medical supplies, food, and water they had on hand, the walls surrounding their convent became the makeshift hospital for over eight hundred people brought to them overnight on stretchers, wheelbarrows, or slung over the shoulders of those strong enough to carry them. With the world around them in shambles, these sisters allowed faith, hope, and love to lead them beyond what their senses were telling them was humanly possible.

This impresses upon us the necessity of bringing order to our senses so that our feet might be pointed in the right direction to be led by Jesus into His rest. The mystics will recognize that "it is the pull of our passions that undermines our peace."[34] Our passions are easily stimulated through what our senses tell them. They often distract us from what faith is trying to say at a deeper level. They "carry us towards what is pleasing and delightful to us, towards what we love. Thus they cause us to avoid what is unpleasant and hurtful, of things we fear or hate."[35]

In regard to prayer, the hermits of old say that prayer is not possible until the passions are quieted. For "what is prayer without silence? How can there be interior silence unless the voice of the passions is stilled?"[36] The passions are "like strident, quarrelsome voices painfully shattering the stillness of the evening."[37]

One of those ancient hermits, Evagrius Ponticus, observed: "A man in chains cannot run. Nor can the mind that is enslaved to passion see the place of spiritual prayer. It is dragged along and tossed by these passion-filled thoughts and cannot stand firm and tranquil."[38] "The man who strives after true prayer must learn to master not only anger and his lust, but must free himself from every thought that is colored by passion."[39]

Jesus understood this all too well. He "did not need anyone to testify about human nature. He himself understood it well" (John 2:25). In order to be led into His rest, Jesus realized that we would first need to deny our passions their rebellious intent to be our master.

[34] A Carthusian, *The Way of Silent Love* (London: Darton, Longman and Todd, 1994), 84.

[35] Ibid.

[36] Ibid.

[37] Ibid.

[38] Evagrius Ponticus, *The Praktikos & Chapters on Prayer* (Kalamazoo, MI: Cistercian, 1981), chapters on prayer, no. 71.

[39] Ibid., no. 53.

Chapter 2

If Anyone Wishes to Come After Me

(Luke 9:23)

The Active Purifications

Jesus made it clear that to follow Him involves a three-step process. The first step is self-denial.

"If anyone wishes to come after me, he must …

- ✠ Deny himself
- ✠ Take up his cross daily
- ✠ Follow me" (Luke 9:23).

Denying ourselves and picking up our cross might not sound like the path to enter into His rest, but Jesus did not give alternative routes. There will always be false prophets suggesting that one can be a disciple of Christ without sacrifice and suffering. Their appeal is similar to all those popular diet plans that suggest that one can have a healthy body without a balanced diet and proper exercise. These methods may be entertained for a season, but to bear lasting fruit, there is no way to avoid the regimen of a balanced diet and proper exercise. Likewise,

"If anyone wishes to come after me, he must deny himself and take up his cross daily" (Luke 9:23).

With this in mind, Jesus asked His first disciples, "Can you drink the cup that I drink?" (Mark 10:38). To drink of the cup is an Old Testament metaphor for accepting God's plan for our life. To accept God's plan requires us to deny all those other schemes floating around our head. Although many people express a desire to enter into His rest, there are relatively few who are willing to drink of the cup.

Jesus realizes that our attraction to Him is often self-serving. We have all kinds of ideas of where we think our time with Him should lead us. James and John evidently thought their time with Jesus should lead to sitting on His right and left in His glory. They went so far as to tell Jesus, "Teacher, we want you to do for us whatever we ask of you" (Mark 10:35).

By allowing their selfish schemes to take the lead in their relationship with Christ, James and John were missing the true beauty of being a disciple — to be with Jesus and follow Him.

The second step of discipleship is to take up our cross daily. The cross by itself couldn't be more forbidding. In fact, as one wise monk recognized, "The only attractive feature of the cross is its relationship to Jesus."[40] Yet there could be no more attractive relationship. If it means embracing a cross so that I might remain with Jesus, then so be it! Amen.

It is worth noting that a cross and a yoke are basically the same form. A yoke is a custom-designed tool for an animal team that places a stronger, experienced animal with a younger, weaker one. This way the brunt of the burden to be hauled is upon the shoulders of the experienced animal so that it might teach the younger one how to move forward together with the load.

40 A Monk, *The Hermitage Within*, 79.

Our Lord realizes that the cross is coming. No one escapes the cross in this life. Some crosses are extremely heavy. There are crosses that will not go away: the death of a loved one, a chronic physical or mental illness, and/or emotional wounds. If we try to carry these crosses on our own, we remain stuck in place. Knowing this, Our Lord invites us, "Take my yoke upon you and learn from me" (Matt. 11:29). With the brunt of the burden on His shoulders, Jesus continues to lead us forward in a way that "you will find rest for your selves" (Matt. 11:29).

None of this can happen without the first step of denying ourselves.

To repeat, if we do not master our passions they "carry us towards what is pleasing and delightful to us, towards what we love. Thus they cause us to avoid what is unpleasant and hurtful, of things we fear or hate."[41] We cannot be led into His rest if we refuse to enter into His yoke.

The Gospel story of The Rich Young Man (Matt. 19:16–30; Mark 10:17–23; Luke 18:18–30) demonstrates how a lack of self-denial keeps us from entering into His rest. The rich young man in the story was a faithful observer of the Mosaic Law. His attraction to Jesus stirred new questions within him concerning the path to eternal life. He approached Our Lord to ask Him the question Pope St. John Paul II considered as essential and unavoidable for the life of every man:[42] "Good teacher, what must I do to inherit eternal life?" (Mark 10:17).

Jesus responded by commanding the young man to observe the commandments. This enabled him to recognize that observing the

[41] A Carthusian, *The Way of Silent Love*, 84.

[42] John Paul II, *Veritatis splendor* (Vatican City: Libreria Editrice Vaticana, 1993), p. 8.

Law is not enough. In the presence of God's only Son, he asks the more telling question: "What do I still lack?" (Matt. 19:20).

When we place ourselves in the presence of God and honestly examine our lives, we recognize a void that an observance of the Law cannot fill.

As St. Augustine explains, "When one is without these crimes (i.e., infractions against the commandments) one begins to lift up one's head towards freedom. But this is only the beginning of freedom, not perfect freedom."[43] The Law is only able to point our feet in the right direction.

There is a temptation to diminish our spiritual life to just another duty to fulfill in order to get what we want from Jesus, as if by performing the bare minimum of the commandments, God will reward us with eternal life. Heaven is for those who love God with "their whole heart, their whole soul, their whole mind, and all their strength" (Mark 12:30).

The rich young man's response to Jesus' invitation to "follow me" reveals how chained he is to what he loves in this world. Within the context of what could have only been just a few minutes, he went from enthusiasm for seeking eternal life to turning his back on Our Lord and walking away in discouragement.

The *Catechism* explains how our human nature has been wounded and weakened by Original Sin.[44] By nature, we are attracted to the good, and by grace we desire to love God in return. However, the effects of Original Sin tempt us to carefully weigh how fully we respond to this inclination to love God with our whole heart, mind, and soul. Our wounded nature tempts us to disproportionately emphasize what we regard as pleasurable in the here and now. We often

[43] St. Augustine, *In Iohannis Evangelium Tractatus*, 41, 10: CCL 36, 363, in John Paul II, *Veritatis splendor*, no. 13.

[44] CCC 405.

end up valuing the passing goods of this earth over the eternal love offered to us by our Heavenly Father. Like the rich young man, we often refuse to be led by the Lord into His rest and depart from His company restless and sad.

In his inaugural homily, Pope Benedict XVI expresses this predicament accurately:

> If we let Christ enter fully into our lives, if we open ourselves totally to Him, are we not afraid that He might take something away from us? Are we not perhaps afraid to give up something significant, something unique, something that makes life so beautiful? Do we not then risk ending up diminished and deprived of our freedom?[45]

These are the precise questions the rich young man began to ask himself when he was invited by Jesus to step beyond the Law and answer the Call. We will all find ourselves asking the same questions as we are awakened to the love of God. We are torn between seeking our true treasure in Heaven and satisfying our selfish desires in the here and now. The passing goods of this world, so alluring and readily accessible, easily distract us. What we lack is purity of heart. Our hearts have become corrupted by disordered loves. This blocks us from appreciating the beauty of what Pope Benedict XVI goes on to conclude:

> If we let Christ into our lives, we lose nothing, nothing, absolutely nothing of what makes life free, beautiful and great. No! Only in this friendship are the

[45] Benedict XVI, Mass of Inauguration Homily.

> doors of life opened wide. Only in this friendship is the great potential of human existence truly revealed. Only in this friendship do we experience beauty and liberation. And so, today, with great strength and great conviction, on the basis of long personal experience of life, I say to you, dear young people: Do not be afraid of Christ! He takes nothing away, and He gives you everything. When we give ourselves to Him, we receive a hundredfold in return. Yes, open, open wide the doors to Christ — and you will find true life.[46]

In order to enter into His rest, we need to open wide the doors to Christ. The "active purifications" help us open the doors.

Taming the Wild Horse

The Carthusians have long been regarded as masters of the "active purifications." The word they use is *asceticism*. Asceticism comes from a Greek word for exercise or training. Asceticism is a word that we will be using rather extensively, and it is helpful to appreciate how it could be easily exchanged with the word *penance*. Penance is exercise or training in self-denial to turn the heart away from sin and toward God.

The Carthusians were founded by St. Bruno in A.D. 1084. They are that rare religious order of whom Pope Innocent XI said in 1688, "*Cartusia numquam reformata quia numquam deformata*" ("The Carthusians never reformed, because they never deformed"). The Carthusians never lost the original vision of their founder. Their authentic practice of asceticism (self-denial) has much to do with this. True self-denial enables us to keep our focus on Christ.

[46] Ibid.

I once spent eight days experiencing their way of life, and I can attest to the austerity of how they live. They eat one meal a day, break up their sleep at midnight to pray, live alone in a cell, sleep on a straw mattress, heat with wood, maintain silence, and many of them wear a hair shirt. Far from producing a bunch of calloused old monks, it is the term "gentlemen" that resounds in their midst. There is a certain peace within them. They are no longer at war with their passions. Their feet are pointed in the direction that will lead them into His rest.

As the Carthusians rightly perceive: "Our passions have a certain autonomy; they are oriented towards their own ends and are activated when one of these ends appears to the senses or in the mind. At the same time, it is in our power to control them, to submit them to reason and the law of God. But this only can be done with tact, gradually, as one would tame a wild horse."[47]

This image of a wild horse is insightful. The obvious temptation is to allow our passions to run as free as a wild horse. Instead of striving to raise our heads towards perfect freedom, we convince ourselves that we are incapable of change. This is the lie we tell ourselves in order to avoid making sacrifices. We often prefer to yield to the pleasure found in our passions rather than master them through self-denial.

By God's grace, we slowly realize that allowing the wild horse to run free leaves our hearts restless. We gradually understand that it is our undisciplined passions that undermine our peace.[48] Abba Zosima in *The Brothers Karamazov* recognized that "the soul has as many masters as it has passions." His words echo the wisdom of St. Peter who taught, "Whatever overcomes a man, to that he is enslaved" (2 Peter 2:19). These words bring us back to the warning God gave to Cain;

[47] A Carthusian, *The Way of Silent Love*, 87.

[48] Ibid., 84.

"Sin is a demon lurking at the door … yet you can be his master" (Gen. 4:7).

The Carthusians rightly describe that "the drama is that of ourselves we are incompetent. We want to love purely, but we also don't want to entirely, not yet."[49] As St. Augustine memorably put it, "Lord give me chastity, but not yet."[50]

The rich young man was not compelled by Our Lord's invitation of love. The glimpse Jesus gave him of seeking his true treasure in Heaven was not enough to persuade him. Such obstinacy in the presence of Pure Love is sure proof that his corrupt heart "demands *ascesis*."[51] In order to restore peace and order within our hearts, these unruly passions need to be tamed. In the Christian context, asceticism helps "put back into place that something in us which should serve but wants to rule. That is to say, it restores that order which has been upset by the Fall."[52]

Conditions for Discipleship

The rich young man was drawn to Jesus and enthusiastic to learn about what was necessary to inherit eternal life. Showing all the marks of a prospective disciple, he even acknowledges the persistent void in his life that his observance of the commandments was not able to fulfill. Here the story takes a tragic turn. Jesus personally invites the rich young man to become a disciple. He is given the same call — "Follow me" — as the first apostles, who immediately responded by leaving everything. But he cannot bring himself to accept the necessary ascetical condition to "sell all that you have and

49 Ibid., 8.

50 St. Augustine, *Confessions*, 145.

51 A Carthusian, *The Way of Silent Love*, 8.

52 A Carthusian, *They Speak by Silences* (London: Darton, Longman and Todd, 1996), 26.

give to the poor" (Matt. 19:21). The "pearl of great price" (Matt. 13:46) stands before the rich young man, but he is unwilling to "sell everything to possess it." It is very telling that what blocks him from becoming a disciple brings him no consolation; "He went away sad" (Matt. 19:22).

St. Bruno spelled out more directly how this unwillingness to take the ascetical step of discipleship can only lead to ruin: "For what could be more perverted, more reckless and contrary to nature and right order, than to love the creature more than the Creator, what passes away more than what lasts forever, or to seek rather the goods of the earth than those of heaven."[53]

St. Bruno's words are a call to true conversion. In his *Introduction to Christianity*, Pope Benedict XVI demonstrates how the two Latin components of *con-version* quite literally mean "with a turn," or more specifically, "turning back."[54] He explained that our natural human inclination is to turn outward to what is visible. We try to find meaning and fulfillment in these earthly, created things that will all pass away "in a blink of an eye" (1 Cor. 15:52). We need to turn inward to see how blind we are if we trust only what we see with our eyes. Without this change of direction, there can be no belief. In the converted eyes of St. Paul, "we do not fix our gaze on what is seen but on what is unseen; for what is seen is transitory, what is unseen lasts forever" (2 Cor. 4:18). To live a life of faith requires a daily task of denying this natural inclination to look for our true fulfillment in the wrong places.

So how might we approach this ascetical step of Christian discipleship?

[53] St. Bruno, "Letter to Raoul Le Verd," trans. A Carthusian, in *The Wound of Love* (London: Darton, Longman and Todd, 1994), 7.

[54] Benedict XVI, Introduction to Christianity (San Francisco: Ignatius Press, 2004), 51.

First, it is important to realize that these unruly passions are very much like a wild horse. We don't just jump up on it to establish ourself as its master. It will quickly and violently buck us off. A wild horse needs to be tamed gradually and with tact. We slowly and surely limit its boundaries. It is the same in the spiritual life; our practice of self-denial must begin gradually. For example, perhaps reading this book will fill you with a desire to spend time in silence with God each day. If you have never prayed a daily holy hour, it wouldn't be wise to start with an hour in silence each day. Within a week or two you will likely get bucked off. It is best to start small and work your way up. Spend fifteen minutes each day in silence. Your wild horse will prove to be a good enough challenge with that. Then as your passions begin to lose their strength and your desire for God increases, so the time spent in silence will naturally increase.

When we sit down to pray, we soon discover that our unruly passions will attempt to drive us away from being recollected at prayer. It is amazing how quickly we remember all our forgotten tasks as soon as we resolve to spend time with God. As we sit down to pray, we might feel compelled to get up and accomplish these tasks and then return to prayer. I have come to learn that if these tasks are from God, they will still be there after the allotted time of prayer. Our wild horse is in need of taming.

The proper intent of asceticism is to create "an emptiness, a listening ear, a heart that is attentive."[55] In order to cultivate a life of prayer, we need interior silence. This silence can only be achieved by stilling the voice of our passions. In the words of the Carthusians, there can be no peace "unless the voice of the passions is stilled."[56]

[55] A Carthusian, *The Way of Silent Love*, 91.

[56] Ibid., 84.

The Means to an End

From the very beginning, it is important to understand that the active purifications are not an end; they are means to a higher goal. As the Carthusians explain, "We do not give an absolute value to penances. They are the means used for an end: following Christ."[57]

Christ did not require fasting for His immediate disciples; "As long as they have the bridegroom with them they cannot fast" (Mark 2:19). The purpose of fasting is to help us remain with Christ. This is important, for it is tempting to approach asceticism with the thought that our personal efforts at self-denial are capable of earning something from God. This is the road to disaster and defeats the whole purpose behind asceticism.

It is tempting to think we can push ourselves down the road to sanctity by taking on harsh penances. A wise old desert axiom advises, "It is not possible for a man to be recalled from his purpose through harshness, because one demon does not drive out another."[58] Harshness is the demon that places the focus on ourselves and not on Christ. If our life of self-denial leads to self-pity, or to begrudge it, or to take pride in it; if it leads to thinking I am "doing more than others," then in vain do we practice self-denial. "In vain is your earlier rising, your going later to rest ... while God pours out blessings upon his beloved in their sleep" (Ps. 127:2).

As St. Thérèse of Lisieux explains, "Sanctity does not consist in this or that practice; it consists in a disposition of heart which makes us humble and little in the arms of God, conscious of our

[57] A Carthusian, *The Call of Silent Love* (London: Darton, Longman and Todd, 1995), 57.

[58] Desert Axiom, in *Spiritual Direction in the Early Christian East*, by Irénée Hausherr (Kalamazoo, MI: Cistercian, 1990), 68.

weakness, and confident to the point of audacity in the goodness of our Father."[59]

The active purifications point our feet in the right direction to help us recognize that "God's grace is sufficient for you, for power is made perfect in weakness" (2 Cor. 12:9). It is all about the heart, and only a "humble, contrite heart" can be led into the rest of experiencing that "God's grace is sufficient for you."

The Carthusians point out that "everything depends on the motivation behind the *ascesis*."[60] The exterior penitential practices of people may be similar, but it is the interior disposition that determines the effect these acts have on their spiritual life. For example, say three friends decide to take the season of Lent seriously this year by skipping a meal every day. One of them does so with the intention of spending that time in prayer and allowing their hunger to remind them of the price Christ paid for their sins. Another has in mind that such a heroic effort will surely be repaid by Our Lord in receiving the upcoming promotion at work. The third is just hoping they can actually do it, and shed a few pounds in the process. It is evident that though their exterior observance of Lent is the same, they will arrive at Easter Sunday with quite different aspirations in their hearts.

Healing, not Destruction

The goal of self-denial "is not the destruction of the passions but their rehabilitation according to a true priority of values."[61] We are trying to tame the wild horse, not kill it. Our practice of asceticism can be the road to sanctity or insanity. It is not by gritting our teeth that the fruits of God begin to flow. God only responds to love.

59 St. Thérèse of Lisieux, *Her Last Converations* (Washington, D.C.: ICS, 1977), 129.

60 A Carthusian, *The Way of Silent Love*, 90.

61 Ibid., 88.

There is time-tested wisdom in the fast prescribed by the Church. It is not a hard or harsh one — three meals a day consisting of two smaller ones that together would not equal the third larger one, with nothing to eat in between. This isn't hard; it isn't meant to be. It is disciplining. Many of us would eat that way on most days. When you do it with the intention of fasting, the wild horse starts to buck. It doesn't like to be disciplined.

The Carthusians remind us that "a human is a creature marked by the disorder of sin. It requires a long and patient struggle to put some order into anarchic (rebellious) desires, and to create a unity in the pursuit of a noble ideal perceived by the intellect."[62] The path to a pure heart is not by suppressing our natural needs or destroying our human passions. St. Irenaeus once proclaimed, "The glory of God is man alive."[63] To be fully alive entails an intimate awareness of our every passion and need, with the resolve to subject each of them to what alone can satisfy: "loving God with our whole heart, mind, and soul."

Left unchecked, our passions actually serve to restrict us, making us less alive. The gluttonous no longer enjoy food. The greedy no longer enjoy material things. The lustful no longer enjoy human intimacy. The slothful no longer enjoy life. The envious no longer enjoy beauty. The angry no longer enjoy virtue. The prideful no longer enjoy serving God.

In letting the wild horse run free, we will not be brought to the refreshing pastures promised by our Good Shepherd (Ps. 23). It is only by entering the yoke of Christ that we will find true refreshment.

So how do we do this in practical terms?

[62] A Carthusian, *The Call of Silent Love*, 164.

[63] St. Irenaeus, *Against Heresies*, ed. Rev. Alexander Roberts, D.D., in *The Ante-Nicene Fathers*, vol. 1 (Grand Rapids, MI: Eerdmans, 1979), bk. 4. 20, 7, p. 490.

Penance in Practical Terms

Timothy Cardinal Dolan, while serving as rector of the North American College in Rome, described penance to us seminarians in very practical terms. He taught three primary ways by which we practice self-denial:[64]

- ✠ Through voluntary acts of mortification
- ✠ In accepting the rejection that necessarily comes from the world for loyalty to the gospel
- ✠ Through gracefully embracing the adversities and sorrows that accompany our earthly life

Since voluntary acts of mortification are the main focus here, let us first briefly address the latter two ways of practicing penance.

Accepting the rejection that necessarily comes from the world for loyalty to the gospel.

"If the world hates you, realize that it hated me first" (John 15:18). "If they persecuted me, they will also persecute you" (John 15:20).

Jesus made it clear that fidelity to Him would entail persecution. In fact, He instructed us to rejoice in such persecution; "Blessed are you when they insult you and persecute you and utter every kind of evil against you (falsely) because of me. Rejoice and be glad, for your reward will be great in heaven" (Matt. 5:11–12). And indeed, the first apostles did just that. After having been flogged for the Faith, "they left the presence of the Sanhedrin, rejoicing that they had been found worthy to suffer dishonor for the sake of the name" (Acts 5:41).

64 Timothy Cardinal Dolan, "Rector's Conference on Penance" (lecture, Pontifical North American College, Rome, March 2, 1997).

I have to admit that my initial interior reaction to being persecuted has never been as pure. I usually start by questioning why I am not being received; after all, I'm just being faithful to Christ. A rector for the North American College once commented that he had never been thrown out of a place for what he had preached, and that thought did not bring him comfort.

In his *Introduction to Christianity,* Pope Benedict XVI observed: "The Christian of today … is not at liberty to remain satisfied with finding out that by all kinds of twists and turns an interpretation of Christianity can still be found that no longer offends anybody."[65]

With keen accuracy, he expressed in an Angelus address the rejection that will necessarily come from the world for fidelity to the gospel:

> Jesus' peace is the result of a constant battle against evil.… Anyone who desires to resist this enemy by remaining faithful to God and to good, must necessarily confront misunderstandings and sometimes real persecutions. All, therefore, who intend to follow Jesus and to commit themselves without compromise to the truth, must know that they will encounter opposition and that in spite of themselves they will become a sign of division between people, even in their own families. In fact, love for one's parents is a holy commandment, but to be lived authentically it can never take precedence over love for God and love for Christ.[66]

65 Benedict XVI, *Introduction to Christianity,* 56.

66 Benedict XVI, Angelus (August 19, 2007).

Gracefully embracing the adversities and sorrows that accompany our earthly life.

Most opportunities of penance will not require any prior consideration; they come quite naturally. St. Thérèse of Lisieux was a champion at gracefully embracing the trials that came as a natural part of her daily life. She mentions her struggle with "a Sister who has the faculty of displeasing me in everything, in her ways, her words, her character, everything seems *very disagreeable* to me."[67] Thérèse resolved to treat her as she would the person she loved the most. She not only prayed for her, but "took care to render her all the services possible . . . giving her my most friendly smile" to the point that the sister came to comment, "What attracts you so much toward me; every time you look at me, I see your smile?"[68]

Our lives are full of such opportunities: when the line is longer than we want it to be, the driving slower, the flight gets delayed or canceled, when it's too hot, too cold, when sickness comes, when unwelcome visitors arrive. These are all opportunities for penance when gracefully embraced. We don't need to go looking for penance; if we live and love, penance will come to us.

So to "strengthen our drooping hands and our weak knees" (Heb. 12:12), to be ready to gracefully embrace these penitential moments of life as active purifications, we do well to incorporate into our spiritual exercises a regular regimen of voluntary acts of mortification.

Voluntary Acts of Mortification

Theologians have explained how voluntary acts of mortification can assist our spiritual growth in these three ways:

67 St. Thérèse of Lisieux, *Story of a Soul*, 222.

68 Ibid., 223.

- ✠ To feel closer to the Passion of Christ
- ✠ To create a vacuum in our life to be filled by Our Lord
- ✠ By denying ourselves a legitimate pleasure, we are trained to refuse illegitimate pleasures

These points merit individual attention.

Voluntary acts of mortification enable us to identify more closely with the Passion of Christ.

The sufferings Christ endured were a voluntary act of His will. "No one takes my life from me, but I lay it down on my own" (John 10:18). He could have chosen to run away from His Passion. But "he emptied himself and took the form of a slave ... obediently accepting even death, death on a cross" (Phil. 2:7–8). Jesus freely chose to unite His will to the Father's: "This is why the Father loves me, because I lay down my life" (John 10:17).

It is critical to appreciate how Jesus' great love for us and ultimately for the Father enabled Him to endure such extreme sufferings. St. Catherine of Siena once observed, "The nails were not enough to hold God-and-Man nailed and fastened on the Cross had Love not held Him there."[69] It was love that held Jesus to the Cross.

The model we are given to imitate is clear: "Christ suffered for you and left you an example to have you follow in his footsteps" (1 Pet. 2:21). Love needs to be the motivating factor behind every voluntary act of self-denial. Our Father does not look so much at the action being performed as He does the heart. "Not as man sees does God see, because man sees the appearance but the LORD looks into

[69] St. Catherine of Siena, *Letter to Monna Agnese,* trans. and ed. Vida di Scudder, in *St. Catherine of Siena as Seen in Her Letters* (London: Dent, 1927), 42.

the heart" (1 Sam. 16:7). Pope St. John Paul II observes: "Following Christ is not an outward imitation, since it touches man at the very depths of his being. Being a follower of Christ means becoming conformed to Him who became a servant even to giving Himself on the Cross."[70]

Our voluntary acts of mortification enable us to identify more closely with the Passion of Christ.

Creating a vacuum or void to be filled by God.

This seems the most widely recognized motive behind the practice of asceticism. I think that it is more accurately described as coming to terms with the void that has always been there. We have been created to be filled by God. The effects of Original Sin tempt us to fill this void with disordered pleasures. Attempting to satisfy every inclination and desire is like the doctor who treats the symptoms without ever addressing the festering infection inside. Seeking consolation in the pleasures of this world is like putting a bandage on a lacerated heart. The external bleeding may be temporarily stopped, but the hemorrhage continues to kill the person inside. God is the Divine Physician capable of healing our soul. We need to remove the bandage for Him to administer the cure.

For example, when I first entered the hermitage, I planned a recreation time on Sunday with an hour of good music during the evening meal. After that first week of solitude, it was a welcome diversion to break the silence with my favorite musical, *Les Misérables*. Later that evening, during the time of Adoration, what comes into my mind, but the music of *Les Misérables*! It didn't stop there. Throughout the rest of the week, every time I sat down to pray, *Les Misérables* came with me. I quickly recognized that it was time to

[70] John Paul II, *Veritatis splendor,* no. 21.

remove the *Les Misérables* bandage so that the Divine Physician might more freely enter this void He created in my heart that was so *miserably* in need to be filled by Him.

Denying ourselves the pleasure found in legitimate goods strengthens us to resist the temptation to yield to illegitimate pleasures.

Without the actual practice of asceticism, "there is a risk of one's (desired) responses remaining wishful thinking."[71] The Carthusians describe how our desired responses require "regular training, that is to say, repeated ascetic exercises, forming good habits that re-order mental processes, that establish control over impulses, and muscles that facilitate the willed attitude."[72]

Our Lord once explained that "no one can serve two masters. He will either hate one and love the other, or be devoted to one and despise the other" (Matt. 6:24). The master we serve does not come about by chance. We need to strengthen those interior muscles that hold us back from where our passions are trying to pull us. By denying ourselves food in fasting, we may more easily reject the temptation to find satisfaction in worldly goods. In carving out time for prayer, our patience increases and we more readily seek God's intercession throughout the day. A life of poverty will free us from material attachments and dispose us to respond more charitably to the needs of others.

These responses do not come overnight. This is why we call it *the virtue of penance*. A virtue is nurtured by what we practice in the flesh. St. Paul described how "I drive my body and train it, for fear that, after having preached to others, I myself should be

71 A Carthusian, *The Call of Silent Love*, 180.

72 Ibid.

disqualified" (1 Cor. 9:27). He clearly understood how necessary it is to deny ourselves the pleasure found in legitimate goods so that we might be strengthened to resist temptation to yield to illegitimate pleasures.

Allow me to add a fourth point, which has already been woven within.

Proper asceticism teaches trust in God's providence.

Through self-denial we come to learn that God truly does provide what is necessary. We can live without that meal. We will survive with a little less sleep. It won't kill us to swallow our pride. As I noted earlier, on most days we could easily go through the day with the fast of the Church and not even think about it. When we actually plan to follow that fast for the love of God, how hungry we seem to get. In that apparent hunger we learn to trust that God does provide what we really need.

"Love One Another as I Love You" (John 15:12)

The active purifications steer us away from the road of wishful thinking and get our feet pointed in the direction of responding with love to Jesus' invitation, "Follow me."

The one fruit, which alone characterizes the right motives in asceticism, is charity. In fact, "without charity, the virtues are merely an illusion."[73]

St. Teresa of Ávila will help us recognize how we can "be certain that the more advanced you see you are in love for your neighbor, the more advanced you will be in the love of God."[74]

[73] Isaiah the Monophysite, in *Spiritual Direction in the Early Christian East*, 59.

[74] St. Teresa of Ávila, *The Interior Castle*, 5.3.8.

The Carthusians complement this idea in describing that "our capacity for welcoming the other is precisely conditioned by our capacity to welcome God."[75]

The active purifications point our feet in the direction of seeing others as God sees them. "To be concerned for others for their own sake, not only in that tiny part of them which touches on my world, that is to say, insofar as the other is part of my world."[76] When we start to see the world as God sees it, we realize that "to have a spiritual life does not restrict our field of vision . . . [but] enlarges it to embrace the whole of reality."[77]

So often we only see others insofar as their lives touch ours. For example, I am interested in the plumber because I need him to fix my faucet. If he fails to show up at the scheduled time, how tempted I am to get angry with him for not doing what I need him to do when he said he would do it. Self-denial will help me to resist that temptation and realize that he, too, is probably having a difficult day. So, when I call him, instead of making him testy by demanding to know where he is, I might ask him how his day is going and be pleasantly surprised by his response.

St. Thomas Aquinas explains how our increasing love for God enables us "to put enmities aside and show love towards [our] neighbor."[78]

How necessary the active purifications are if we are intent upon entering into His rest. These rousing words of St. Paul are a fitting close to this chapter on the active purifications:

[75] A Carthusian, *The Call of Silent Love*, 66.

[76] A Carthusian, *The Way of Silent Love*, 104.

[77] A Carthusian, *The Call of Silent Love*, 92.

[78] St. Thomas Aquinas, *Summa Theologica*, trans. Fathers of the English Dominican Province (Westminster, MD: Christian Classics, 1981), II-II, q. 28 art. 8, p. 1286.

I urge you therefore, brothers, by the mercies of God, to offer your bodies as a living sacrifice, holy and pleasing to God, your spiritual worship. Do not conform yourselves to this age but be transformed by the renewal of your mind, that you may discern what is the will of God, what is good and pleasing and perfect. (Rom. 12:1–2)

Chapter 3

Remain in My Love

John 15:9

Christian Prayer

Having our passions on the happy road of rehabilitation, we find ourselves better equipped to enter into prayer. Our heart is now more ready to listen, and our feet are pointed in the right direction to be led into His rest.

The disciples witnessed the profound intimacy of Jesus' dialogue with the Father and asked Him to teach them to pray. They were likely looking for something concrete. We too might desire some concrete steps toward receiving the gift of contemplative prayer. But precise steps are difficult to mark off for entering into intimacy with God; it would be like trying to teach someone how to fall in love. The path to "remain in my love" will differ slightly from person to person. Some will find the process more difficult than others. Prayer was never meant to be complicated; in fact, it is very simple. That doesn't mean it is always easy. Nevertheless, we have a tendency to make it much more difficult than it needs to be.

To illustrate this point, I will relate a story about Harry Houdini, the great escape artist, as told by Fr. Paul Murray, O.P., a professor of mine at the Angelicum University in Rome. In his time, Houdini was the master of escaping from practically anything. An event was set up to display the mastery of his skills. A maze of thirty different contraptions was devised for him to escape from in thirty minutes. The media was eager to see if Houdini was actually that good. He was. In fact, he escaped from the first twenty-nine contraptions with plenty of time to spare. Then he came to the last lock, a simple door lock, by far the easiest within the maze. To everyone's bewilderment, he stood by this door trying to pick the lock for a longer time than any of the previous twenty-nine contraptions. Finally, well within the allotted time, Houdini came through to the other side. All were quick to laud him on this amazing feat. The media couldn't help but focus on the problem he had with that last simple lock. Houdini's reply: "I always work under the assumption that the door is locked." The Great Houdini was standing before an unlocked door trying to pick it open.

We are prone to approach prayer similarly, as if God set prayer before us as a challenge to unlock the fountain of His love. We are prone to place too much emphasis on our own efforts. God doesn't need to be *found*. He has already revealed Himself. There is harm in imagining God to be far away.

Prayer is much simpler than we might dare to imagine. Perhaps we are familiar with the picture depicting the passage from the book of Revelation in which Jesus stands at the door and knocks (3:20). The secret in this picture is that the door Jesus is knocking on has no handle on His side. The handle is on our side.

So here is our first principle of prayer — the door is not locked, and the handle is on our side.

"Remain in My Love" (John 15:9)

These words reveal the great goal of every human vocation. God loves us, and He has invited us to remain in His love, now and forever. We are not the initiators of this relationship of love; we are responders:

- ✠ "In this is love: not that we have loved God, but that he loved us" (1 John 4:10).
- ✠ "We love because he first loved us" (1 John 4:19).

God loves us. It is His great desire that we remain in His love. If the relationship falters, it is because of our lack of resolve to respond to His love with our whole heart, our whole mind, and our whole soul. God, for His part, is continually trying to woo us into an intimate relationship. His love for us never fails. The door to intimacy with Him is unlocked, but the handle is on our side.

So, how do we begin to open the doors of our hearts and allow Him to enter and remain?

Before I continue, I realize that due to different cultural backgrounds or past wounds, it can sometimes be difficult to appreciate the human terms of marital intimacy that will be used to describe our relationship with God. So, I hope you will understand that it is the language of the Church to speak of God as a Spouse, His touch as a kiss, our ultimate goal with Him as union, and some experiences of prayer as ecstasy. This is the language used in Sacred Scripture and by the mystics. God's love is truly beyond what we can describe in human terms, so these terms are not necessary for coming to know that "God is love" (1 John 4:16). Yet we will spend time with them, for in the wisdom of the Church they have been found beneficial to describe our relationship with the God of love.

"God is love, and whoever remains in love remains in God and God in him" (1 John 4:16).

God is love. A relationship with God is a relationship of love. Prayer is how we enter, express, and experience this love. St. Bernard of Clairvaux wrote eighty-six sermons on the Song of Songs. Now that is a man in love! In the eighty-third sermon, he describes the different degrees of love:

> Love is a great reality; but there are degrees to it. The bride stands at the highest. Children love their father, but they are thinking of their inheritance, and as long as they have any fear of losing it, they honor more than they love the one from whom they expect to inherit. I hold in suspect the love which seems to be founded on some hope of gain. It is weak, for if the hope is removed, it may be extinguished, or at least diminished. It is not pure, as it desires some return. Pure love has no self-interest. Pure love does not gain strength through expectation, nor is it weakened by distrust. This is the love of the bride, for this is the bride, with all that it means to be a bride. Love is the being and the hope of a bride. She is full of love, and the bridegroom is contented with it. He asks nothing else, and she has nothing else to give. That is why He is the bridegroom and she is the bride; this love is the property only of the couple. No one else can share it, not even a son.[79]

The relationship that is being held out to us with the Bridegroom is beyond that of even a son or daughter. This is the depth of intimacy Jesus prayed we might enter, "that they may all be one, as you, Father, are in me and I in you, that they also may be in us," (John 17:21) "that the love with which you loved me may be in them and I in them" (v. 26).

So how do we enter into love with God as His bride and remain in His love? In my opinion, it is not unlike a human romantic relationship.

[79] St. Bernard of Clairvaux, *On the Song of Songs*, vol. 4 (Kalamazoo, MI: Cistercian, 1980), 184–185.

In a relationship of human love, one of the parties begins by showing an interest. Johnny sees Susie across the room and is attracted to her. He may start asking some of her friends about her. He could admire her from a distance, talk about her, and express how much he would like to get to know her. But for the relationship to actually begin, he will eventually need to talk to her.

In the relationship of divine love, God makes the initiative. He intentionally attracts us to Him through the beauty and wonder of His creation. We might ask other people what they think about the Creator of Heaven and earth. We might admire God from a distance. To actually enter into a relationship with Him, we will eventually need to talk with God. We call this *vocal prayer*.

Vocal Prayer

Through words, mental or vocal, our prayer takes flesh. Vocal prayer is the beginning of the encounter with God. We become aware of whom we are addressing. For our words to be truly prayer, they must come from the heart. The very purpose of prayer is to open our hearts to God. On this point, St. John Chrysostom states, "Whether your prayer is heard depends not on the number of words, but on the fervor of our souls."[80]

So how fervent are our vocal prayers? I can only speak for myself, but I sometimes fall into that hypocritical mode Jesus warned of in thinking I am being heard because of the mere words I am saying (Matt. 6:7). It is important to appreciate that those words are really more for me than they are for God. God knows my every thought before it is spoken (Ps. 139:4). The words are there to express what is in my heart. God already knows what is happening in my heart. Like any lover or good father, He still likes to hear it come from our own mouths.

[80] St. John Chrysostom, *Ecloga de oratione* 2: PG 63, 585, in CCC 2700.

One of the shortest prayers in the Catholic tradition is the Sign of the Cross. Those words and motions are there to open my heart to whom I am talking. I am now addressing the Father, the Son, and the Holy Spirit, who loved me to the point of having our Father send His Son to die on the Cross. It is a beautiful prayer to open my heart to God. It is a prayer we pray so often that we can easily fall into the habit of saying it perfunctorily: "InthenameoftheFather andoftheSonandoftheHolySpirit." Did that just open my heart? Or was I just going through a routine?

An elderly man in the parish I was serving would arrive each morning for Mass, pause at the baptismal font, dip his hand into the holy water, and look straight up at the crucifix as he reverently signed himself while praying, "In the name of the Father, and of the Son, and of the Holy Spirit. Amen." It was good for me to see, especially since I can sometimes be rather critical of the vocal response of prayer from the congregation in our celebration of Mass. For example, in the preface of the Eucharistic Prayer, the priest begins by saying, "The Lord be with you." They respond, "And with your spirit." I often question if they really mean it. Did those words really express what is in their heart? The sheer lack of emotion leaves me unconvinced that they really wanted the Lord to be with me.

It gets worse. "Lift up your hearts." They respond, "We lift them up to the Lord." At that point I am often tempted to stop the routine dialogue because the response can be so muffled and depressing that I have a hard time believing their hearts were being lifted up. These are the ramblings of a weak pastor. I am simply trying to make a point of the trap we too often carelessly fall into, to cease praying vocally as the words fail to come from the heart.

There is a story, and I am pretty sure it is true, of a pastor who wanted to make this point with the parish he was serving. At the time of the Apostles' Creed, he decided to test the congregation by using other words Americans have memorized for when we stand up together. As they all rose, he began, "I pledge allegiance to the flag of the United States of America, and to the republic for which it stands." They all followed. He could barely contain himself in pointing out that they were not praying the Apostles' Creed, but reciting the Pledge of Allegiance! We need to take care to ensure that our words to God are indeed vocal prayers by having them truly come from our heart.

Although vocal prayer is the initial stage of prayer, it is worth noting that vocal prayer is the form Jesus Himself taught us. We never become so advanced in prayer that we cease to pray vocally. Just as in a good marriage, the couple never moves beyond the need to communicate verbally. In our humanity, we need to express our feelings externally.

Now back to that relationship between Johnny and Susie. At the initial stage of their relationship, they will engage in all kinds of verbal communication. They will seemingly never tire of talking with and listening to one another. When they aren't able to communicate directly, they will often reflect on their conversations of the past. They might even exchange letters and photos of each other in their desire to keep the communication flowing. Remember those love letters one never tires of reading over and over again?

The same principle is at work in the relationship of divine love. The beginning stages are full of vocal prayer. Then we will likely begin to read from the great eternal love letter: Sacred Scripture. It is a letter we never tire of reading and gleaning something new from with every opening of the Word. We might even enhance our appreciation of what is written by reflecting on some image that depicts what is being read. We call this type of prayer *meditation*.

Meditation

Meditation is also referred to as mental prayer. Meditation is taking the conversation we began vocally with Our Lord and continuing it in our mind. As St. Teresa of Ávila explained, "Mental prayer in my opinion is nothing else than an intimate sharing between friends; it means taking time frequently to be alone with Him who we know loves us."[81]

Meditation is our initial effort to listen to God. In vocal prayer we did all the talking. In meditation, we make the effort in our mind to reflect on the path God is calling us to follow. We use our imagination to reflect on what God has revealed and how we are called to respond to His revelation. In the prayer of meditation, we are aided by Sacred Scripture (especially the Gospels), holy icons, and spiritual readings. Religious images are also a common aid for meditation. Our use of them can be misleading to those outside the Catholic tradition, for we do not actually pray to a crucifix or a statue. These are mere images that lead us deeper into the mystery of whom we are addressing in prayer. It is a very human element of prayer, similar to our use of photos of loved ones. In kissing a photograph of my mother, I am not thinking that I am actually kissing her. It is simply that her image evokes in me a desire to express my affection for her in a human way.

Meditation is still very much the activity of a man or a woman in his or her mind. We might say that it is as far as we can go on our own initiative. It is not purely our initiative; God still needs to give us the grace to engage in vocal prayer and meditation. The next step in prayer, however, is not one we are able to engage in at will.

Back to Johnny and Susie. If matters continue to progress, Johnny and Susie will likely desire to communicate their affection for one another in a way that words are unable to express. They will desire to enter into a kiss. I am no expert on the matter, so I asked our diaconate candidates and their wives, and they assure me that it is not possible to kiss and talk at the same time. For the kiss to happen, the talking

[81] St. Teresa of Ávila, *The Collected Works of St. Teresa of Ávila, The Book of Her Life*, chap. 8, par 5.

necessarily stops. Furthermore, if the kiss is to be an authentic communication of love, it cannot be forced. Johnny can't grab Susie to plant one on her lips. If Johnny wants to enter into a kiss with Susie, the best he can do is purse his lips and hope she responds.

In the Song of Songs, we hear of the bride's burning desire for God to "kiss me with the kisses of his mouth" (1:2). Our great desire in prayer is to be kissed by God. For that kiss to happen, the vocal prayer needs to take a rest, if only for the moment. God's great desire to kiss us is often frustrated by our unwillingness to stop talking in prayer. This kiss will also never happen if we try to make it happen. The best we can do is to remain in silence and wait for God to respond.

This kiss of God we call *contemplation*.

Contemplative Prayer

Contemplative prayer is the pure activity of God. Contemplation is something we can only be disposed to receive, just like the kiss. One hermit rightly observed how "you cannot be a mystic for the asking."[82] God gives the gift of contemplative prayer when He sees fit.

In St. Teresa of Ávila's *The Interior Castle* she describes in the third dwelling those who regularly practice meditation. She remarks that some can remain here their whole lives, convinced they have reached the top of the mountain. Christian prayer needs to go further.

Pope St. John Paul II made the distinction between contemplative prayer as described by St. John of the Cross, and the method of prayer taught in Buddhism. He was responding to many in our Western culture who are fascinated by the teachings of Buddha. Some have come to regard its ascetic and mystical techniques as an alternative or a complement to Christianity. Pope St. John Paul II's

[82] A Monk, *The Hermitage Within*, 27.

wise response: "Carmelite mysticism begins at the point where reflections of Buddha end."[83]

The reflections of Buddha, he explains, are an effort "to liberate ourselves only through detachment from the world."[84] It is a method of prayer focused on our effort to become indifferent to a world we have come to consider bad. Christian mysticism, on the other hand, "is not born of a purely negative 'enlightenment.' It is not born of an awareness of the evil that exists in man's attachment to the world through the senses, the intellect, and the spirit. Instead, Christian mysticism is born of the Revelation of the living God. This God opens Himself to union with man, arousing in him the capacity to be united with Him, especially by means of the theological virtues — faith, hope, and above all, love."[85]

The world God created is good. Yet we have been created for something better!

The ordinary path to contemplation is through *the dark night*, when God makes it impossible for us to meditate as He tries to free us from our attachment to lesser goods. This does not mean to suggest that there is something wrong with meditation and vocal prayer; the door is simply being opened to contemplation. This is that breaking point in prayer spoken of in the introduction, which serves to separate the mere activity of man from the pure activity of God.

This is the process we are about to go through, step-by-step.

The three expressions of prayer found in the *Catechism* have now been spelled out for us: vocal prayer, meditation, and contemplation. Let us open our hearts to understanding contemplative prayer as St. John of the Cross understood it.

83 John Paul II, *Crossing the Threshold of Hope* (UK: Random House, 1994), 87.
84 Ibid., 86.
85 Ibid., 87–88.

The following description of contemplative prayer, written by St. John of the Cross, is a real gem. We will hear it again when we cover chapter ten in book one of *The Dark Night*. For now, it will be our basis for understanding this beautiful gift of God.

"Contemplation is nothing else than a secret and peaceful and loving inflow of God, which, if not hampered, fires the soul in the spirit of love."[86]

Contemplation is "secret"

Contemplation is the height of Christian prayer and is open to all — no locks. This gift of God comes quite secretly, without us knowing how it happens. It does not come through the activity of our mind, as in meditation. It remains so secret that St. Teresa of Ávila comments that the faculties are "looking in wonder at what they see."[87]

We may have experienced something of contemplation long before we studied how to pray. It is not unusual for a child to experience this "secret and peaceful and loving inflow of God." Jesus did teach us our need to become like children (Matt. 18:3). Children don't need to understand why they are receiving the gifts they are given. They readily accept them, even when they don't deserve them. Contemplation is a gift we could never earn. It requires humility to receive this gift that comes in such a mysterious way. Contemplation is "secret."

Contemplation is "peaceful"

When St. John Vianney observed the daily devotion of a peasant in Ars who would come and sit for some quiet, peaceful moments in the church, he asked what he was doing. The poor man responded: "I look at Him and He looks at me."

86 St. John of the Cross, *The Dark Night,* 1.10.6.

87 St. Teresa of Ávila, *The Interior Castle,* 4.2.6.

Contemplation is the silent, peaceful gaze known between lovers. We might call it the language of lovers.

Contemplation is not unlike being fluent in a foreign language. I lived in Italy for four years while studying for the priesthood and needed to learn some Italian. What I learned was an exhausting process of translation. I would hear what was said in Italian and try to translate it in my head into English. If I needed to reply, I would need to think of it in English and then translate it into Italian.

There is another level at which a foreign language can be appreciated. When one is fluent, no translation is necessary. It comes peacefully.

Vocal prayer and meditation are not unlike the process of translation. In vocal prayer we take what we know in human terms and try to express them to the Divine. In meditation we attempt to take what has been divinely revealed and translate it into what we can humanly grasp.

In contemplation no translation is necessary. It comes peacefully. We are now fluent in the silent language of God.

To distinguish between meditation and contemplation St. Teresa of Ávila used the image of water filling a trough. In meditation "the water comes from far away through many aqueducts and the use of much ingenuity; with the other, the source of water is right there, and the trough fills without any noise."[88] Contemplation is "peaceful."

Contemplation is "loving"

I was once asked to describe contemplation in a way that a married couple could easily comprehend. It struck me that contemplation is very much like the kiss one might enter into with one's spouse. In a kiss, there is a presence of love that is beyond the capacity of what one person alone could experience. Alone, we could talk about what

[88] Ibid., 4.2.3.

a great thing it would be to kiss; we might try to describe a past experience of a kiss; we might make the effort to explain what it would mean to kiss. All these efforts utterly fail to produce the experience of the actual kiss.

In the same way, we might talk in vocal prayer about what a great thing it is to love and be loved by God. Through meditation we could try to imagine a past experience of such love, but it all pales when compared to the actual kiss received in contemplation.

Contemplation is the experience of God's love that is beyond our capacity to produce alone. It is beyond what we alone can do in meditation. When this kiss of God is authentically experienced, St. John of the Cross said, "A little of this pure love is more precious to God and the soul and more beneficial to the Church, even though it seems one is doing nothing, than all these other works put together."[89]

This is important to bear in mind, as it might seem like a big waste of time to sit and wait for a kiss. In love, there is always a risk. Married couples take a risk of believing their spouse's promise of love. Entering into silent prayer requires a risk—Jesus might not come as I expect. It is a risk to deny ourselves the consolation we find in vocal prayer and meditation. To "be still and know that I am God" (Ps. 46:11) is the risk made in the loving conviction that the "one who made the promise is worthy of trust" (Heb. 11:11). Contemplation is "loving."

Contemplation must be left "not hampered"

There is a story of a man who was to give an acceptance speech for an award being presented to him by his parish. The man was at the

[89] St. John of the Cross, *The Collected Works of St. John of the Cross, The Spiritual Canticle,* stanza 29, par. 2.

head table seated beside the parish priest. Just prior to the presentation, his wife passed him a note. As he opened the note, he smiled as he saw the letters "K.I.S.S." with no other notations. The parish priest caught a glimpse of this and remarked to the man how precious it was that his wife would encourage him with a kiss before his speech, to which the man responded, "It isn't what you think, Father; those letters are an acronym that stands for 'Keep It Simple, Stupid.'"

Good advice for those longing to receive the kisses of His mouth (Song of Sol. 1:2): Keep It Simple, Sinners.

In asking us to "be still," a very simple request is being made of us. Resist the urge to hamper the activity of God by getting busy with your own activity in prayer. St. Teresa of Ávila advises, "Doing something arduous would cause more harm than good ... leave the soul in God's hands, let Him do whatever He wants with it."[90]

Try your best to follow the example of the peasant of Ars and just keep looking at Him while He looks at you. The author of *The Cloud of Unknowing* echoes the utter importance of the simple act of pure love in contemplative prayer we just heard from St. John of the Cross. "One loving, blind desire for God alone is more valuable in itself, more pleasing to God and to the saints, more beneficial to your own growth, and more helpful to your friends, both living and dead, than anything else you could do."[91] Contemplation must be left "not hampered."

Contemplation "fires the soul in a spirit of love"

When a soul is given the gift of contemplative prayer, it will bear the fruit of two beautiful virtues: humility and charity. Humility is born from an awareness that a gift of God's love has been received that is

[90] St. Teresa of Ávila, *The Interior Castle*, 4.3.6.

[91] *The Cloud of Unknowing* (Garden City, NY: Image Books, 1973), chap. 9, p. 60.

way beyond our ability to earn. This, in turn, "fires [our] soul in a spirit of love." Since we have received a gift we could not earn, we are now on fire to be more charitable to our neighbor.

St. Teresa assures us, "Be certain that the more advanced you see you are in love for your neighbor, the more advanced you will be in the love of God."[92]

This fire of love that ignites in a soul through contemplation is much safer than the flames of other spiritual gifts that can be fanned at the level of our senses. St. Paul teaches, "If I speak in human and angelic tongues but do not have love, I am a resounding gong or a clashing cymbal. And if I have the gift of prophecy and comprehend all mysteries and all knowledge; if I have all faith so as to move mountains but do not have love, I am nothing" (1 Cor. 13:1–2).

The gifts of tongues, prophecies, healing, and the like are all ways in which our senses can be awakened to the presence of God. These gifts are meant to lead us to a life in the spirit. In many cases they do just that.

It can also happen that these extraordinary gifts will have us thinking we are at the top of the mountain in the spiritual life. What is sometimes promoted as a "life in the spirit" often has much more to do with what is being experienced in the senses. Tongues and prophecies are spoken and heard; healings affect our sense of touch. St. John of the Cross will help us appreciate how our attachment to such extraordinary experiences will need to be purified in order to be led to a true life in the spirit. We need to go beyond "what eye can see and ear can hear."

I was once challenged by a man who asserted his belief that the Church had lost sight of her power to heal. He had just been part of a healing service in which many people were being cured of physical

92 St. Teresa of Ávila, *The Interior Castle*, 5.3.8.

ailments. He asked me point blank if I had ever healed anyone. I responded that I had that very morning. He excitedly exclaimed, "So you have the gift of healing! What did you do?" My response, "I absolved a soul of their sins." He despondently remarked, "Oh, that." My response: "Yes, *that*!"

I reminded him of Our Lord's immediate response to the paralyzed man. It was not the healing of his body that Jesus was most concerned with; it was the forgiveness of his sins (Matt. 9:1–8). The Church has not lost sight of the true power of Christ's healing. The physical healings are signs that Jesus is the Christ (Matt. 11:4–6), and we all know how Jesus regarded those who kept asking for signs (Matt. 12:39). Let us not become so impressed by the signs of Christ's presence that we miss the whole purpose of what it means to have the Christ now dwelling with us. He has come to heal our souls.

St. John the Evangelist warns us to "not trust every spirit but test the spirits to see whether they belong to God" (1 John 4:1). Are these gifts leading one to a life in the spirit, or are they trapping one in an experience of their senses? One could easily become more inclined to attend a healing service than to receive the Sacrament of Reconciliation, to pray in tongues rather than to receive Holy Communion in Mass.

The evil one can use such experiences to lure us into spiritual pride. I remember hearing a spiritual director forbid his directee to use the gift of healing. For although other people were being healed of physical ailments, his own soul was swelling with pride. In charismatic prayer groups, there can be a similar temptation to pride in drawing a line between who is receiving a particular gift and who is not.

Within the authentic tradition, *charismata,* the Greek term for "gifts of grace," are recognized as "extraordinary, supernatural, and transitory gifts given directly for the common good."[93] In the words of the *Catechism*: " 'God is Love' and love is his first gift, containing all others."[94] A true charismatic is one who receives gifts of love from God and uses them for the good of all. One of the signs of an authentic gift of the Spirit of God is that we are not in control of them. God remains the giver who gives them when He wants. Contemplation is the highest gift of the Spirit of God that will know no end. Contemplation cannot be brought about by our own will. An authentic reception of this gift "fires the soul in a spirit of love" that reaches out to one's neighbor.

As St. Paul advises, in the end it will not be about tongues, prophecies, and the like: "Faith, hope, love remain, these three; but the greatest of these is love" (1 Cor. 13:13).

Contemplation "fires the soul in a spirit of love."

Prepared for the Kiss

We are now prepared to allow St. John of the Cross and St. Teresa of Ávila to walk us down that ordinary path by which they received most deeply the kiss of contemplation. In human terms, what they describe is well beyond the image of a kiss. It is union with God they speak of.

Before we go step-by-step through *The Interior Castle* and *The Dark Night*, it might be worth reflecting on the union God is calling us into with Him. Jesus beautifully expresses His desire "that they may be one, as you, Father, are in me and I in you, that they also may be in us" (John 17:21).

Like many mystics, St. Teresa of Ávila and St. John of the Cross draw upon the truth that there are only two relationships in which we

93 *The Catholic Source Book*, ed. Rev. Peter Klein, (Dubuque: Brown-ROA, 1990), 69.

94 CCC 733.

are able to validly speak of two becoming one: between a man and woman in marriage, and the union we seek with God.

Marital union is the image we are given to understand the reality of our union with God. The Old Testament is no stranger to using our human experience of marital love to help grasp the spiritual nature of our relationship with God. The prophecies of Hosea (2:16–22), Ezekiel (16:6–14) and Isaiah (54:4–6) all use the metaphor of a marriage to describe the relationship between God and His people.

The New Testament is also very familiar with this image. The book of Revelation describes the Second Coming of Christ as the "wedding day of the Lamb" (Rev. 19:7). Jesus compares the kingdom of Heaven to a wedding feast (Matt. 22:1–14) and warns us to be ready to greet the bridegroom (Matt. 25:1–13). St. Paul does not miss this reference as he sets Christ before us as our one true husband (2 Cor. 11:2) and likens the relationship between Christ and the Church to that of a marriage (Eph. 5:23).

God has chosen marital love as the image for us to begin to appreciate the intimacy He longs to lead us into with Him. The experience of marital love will be an effective tool for many to learn what it means to love and be loved on earth as they hope to love and be loved in Heaven. There are also those who are called to "renounce marriage for the sake of the kingdom of God" (Matt. 19:12). These bear witness to the reality of how the true, lasting union we seek is not in marriage. Jesus explains, "At the resurrection they neither marry nor are given in marriage but are like the angels in heaven" (Matt. 22:30).

Marital union is the image we are given to understand the reality of our union with God. Union with God is the ultimate reality we seek. The difference between the two is like seeing a picture of the

Bahamas and going to the Bahamas. One is the image; the other is the reality.

The intimacy experienced between husband and wife will always remain our clearest reference point on earth for describing intimacy with God. Virgin mystics have found it natural to resort to such terms as ecstasy and espousal to describe their experience of union with Him. One of those virgin mystics, St. Teresa of Ávila, while commenting on the Song of Songs, realized some people have difficulty with such romantic language in reference to our relationship with God. Some went so far as to suggest that we not listen to those passages of Sacred Scripture that make blatant use of it. She warns that, "Just as poisonous creatures turn everything they eat into poison, so do we."[95] In other words, we often come with poisoned minds to the Word of God.

If you were the evil one, would you not focus all your energy in trying to tarnish and destroy the very image we are given to appreciate God's love for us? In addressing the topic of human sexuality, St. John Chrysostom once chided his listeners: "Why do you blush? Is it not pure? You are behaving like heretics!"[96] Far from being something naughty, the marital embrace is sacred.

There was no blushing in Pope St. John Paul II as he unveiled an in-depth understanding of the beauty of marital love in a volume of work we now recognize as the *Theology of the Body*. Some were shocked to hear a priest speak so directly about the experience of human sexuality. His wisdom was of one who had gone well beyond the image and into an experience of the reality of union with God.

[95] St. Teresa of Ávila, *The Collected Works of St. Teresa of Ávila, Meditations on the Song of Songs,* chap.1, par. 3.

[96] St. John Chrysostom, *Twelfth Homily on the Epistle to the Colossians,* in *The Four Cardinal Virtues,* by Josef Pieper (Notre Dame, IN: University of Notre Dame Press, 1966), 155.

While I was preparing a retreat on the Gospel of John, I was also reading a condensed version of the *Theology of the Body*. This vast volume had been effectively summarized by four basic characteristics of marital love. The love between a man and woman that reaches out to the dignity God extends to them in the Sacrament of Marriage must be free, total, faithful, and fruitful.

As I continued to prepare the retreat material on the Gospel of John, it struck me that these same four characteristics are true of the way Christ loves us. Then in prayer it dawned on me that this is also the manner in which I am called to love Him. When these four characteristics are true for me in prayer, the kiss of contemplation will not be far off.

In order to better appreciate these four characteristics of love, let us review how they are true of marital love. Then we will listen to how Jesus makes them characteristic of His love in the Gospel of John. Finally, we will apply them to how they should mark our time spent in prayer.

Marital Love: Free, Total, Faithful, Fruitful

In determining whether a man and woman have the proper disposition for marriage, the Church sets before them three questions within the liturgical celebration of the Sacrament of Matrimony. They are posed to help clarify their understanding of marital love. In preparing couples for marriage, I found it quite helpful to use these questions as the basis of our preparation.

1) Have you come here to enter into Marriage without coercion, freely and wholeheartedly?

Marital love must be free. One cannot feel coerced or manipulated into marriage. There is a term called a "shotgun wedding." This was when the couple became pregnant before any formal proposals were made. The father of the bride then made an offer his prospective son-in-law could not refuse. But marital love must be free. That is why we often have an expecting couple wait until after the child is born before celebrating any sacrament. Even within marriage, if the marital embrace is not entered into freely, it can be denigrated into a form of rape or prostitution.

The characteristic of being total is also encompassed within the question of giving yourselves freely and wholeheartedly. Nothing can be held back or kept hidden in your total gift of self within marriage. Your whole heart needs to be in it. This is why prenuptial agreements are not allowed within the Sacrament of Matrimony. It holds something back just in case this doesn't work out and negates the totality necessary to celebrate this gift of God's love.

This is also why the use of contraception cannot be allowed within the act of marital love. Contraception says, "I give you everything except my fertility. We don't want that right now, so let's keep it hidden." Marital love must be total.

2) Are you prepared, as you follow the path of Marriage, to love and honor each other for as long as you both shall live?

Marital love must be faithful. "For as long as you both shall live" means exactly what it says. To prosper, the human family relies on marital fidelity. Children should not be unnecessarily deprived of having both parents.

It is also worth noting here that a man's body and a woman's body are so designed that to engage in the sexual act with more than one partner exposes oneself to the infection of very serious and even deadly diseases. Marital love must be faithful.

3) Are you prepared to accept children lovingly from God and to bring them up according to the law of Christ and His Church?

Fruitfulness is the final characteristic of authentic marital love. Marital love must be open to children. To accept children lovingly from God:

accept, not take. That means if God gives you zero children or twenty-five, you accept, lovingly. St. Catherine of Siena was the twenty-fourth child of twenty-five. We might have remarked to the Benincasa family at number twenty that they had done their job in being open to accepting children. Had they stopped there, we would have only three female doctors in the Church, and the pope might still be in France, as St. Catherine was instrumental in having the papacy return to Rome. Those are two fruits we wouldn't want to be without.

From day one of Creation, children have been regarded as a blessing from God. Today it seems they are almost considered a curse. Contraception tells God how many children we will take. Imagine coming before Our Lord on the Day of Judgment and having Him reveal that, although He appreciates the beautiful love you have shown your three children, He did have four, five, and six planned. These are souls that will never exist, not on earth or in Heaven. I am thankful that my parents were open to number four. Marital love must be fruitful.

Christ's Love: Free, Total, Faithful, Fruitful

In the context of the Gospel of John, these same four characteristics of love are exemplified in the love of Jesus Christ. I will let Jesus speak for Himself on this point.

Free: "No one takes my life from me, but I lay it down on my own" (John 10:18).

Total: "No one has greater love than this, to lay down one's life for one's friends" (John 15:13).

Faithful: "Amen, amen, I say to you, a son cannot do anything on his own, but only what he sees his father doing" (John 5:19). "This is why the Father loves me, because I lay down my life" (John 10:17). "I am troubled now. Yet what should I say? 'Father, save me from this hour?' But it was for this purpose that I came to this hour" (John 12:27).

Fruitful: "Unless a grain of wheat falls to the ground and dies, it remains just a grain of wheat; but if it dies, it produces much fruit" (John 12:24). "Whoever believes in me will do the works that I do, and will do greater ones than these, because I am going to the Father" (John 14:12). "It is for your own good that I am going, because unless I go, the Paraclete will not come to you; But if I go, I will send him to you" (John 16:7).

The love of Jesus Christ is free, total, faithful, and fruitful.

(On the last point of being fruitful, I have often reflected on how strangely true it is that we will do greater earthly works than Jesus. Jesus fed thousands; St. Teresa of Calcutta and her sisters have certainly fed more. Jesus preached to crowds of thousands; Pope St. John Paul II preached to millions.)

Contemplative Prayer: Free, Total, Faithful, Fruitful

The map has been carefully made of the four characteristics of love so that we have a working tool with which we can consider our efforts in prayer. These four characteristics help discern if our time spent in prayer is an act of true love. If the kiss of contemplation is not happening, one of these four characteristics will have likely fallen into neglect.

Free: Contemplative prayer does not come to one who prays out of mere obligation.

Our decision to pray must be entered into freely. To be free in prayer also means that we have no expectations of God during that time. We often enter prayer with ulterior motives. That is why we get frustrated with dryness, find it difficult to remain committed to times of silence, and become interested in trying to somehow measure our progress. Contemplative prayer comes only to those who freely seek Him "whom my soul loves" (Song of Sol. 1:7).

Total: Contemplative prayer will only happen when we give ourselves totally to God.

We can be tempted to hide parts of our life from God and present to Him in prayer who we are at our best. For example, when I used to play golf, it wasn't uncommon to be asked what I shoot. For some reason, I would be tempted to tell them my best score. Then people would go out golfing with me and realize that I am not really that good.

Sometimes in prayer I can be tempted to present myself before God as I am at my best. God, however, has been with me all day long. He knows me through and through. For contemplative prayer to happen, I need to give myself to Him as I totally am, wholeheartedly. Every distraction, agenda, thought, idea, sin, and success must be given to Him — totally.

Faithful: Contemplative prayer requires our fidelity.

These words from the *Catechism* address this point well: "The choice of the *time and duration of the prayer* arises from a determined will, revealing the secrets of the heart. One does not undertake contemplative prayer only when one has the time: one makes time for the Lord, with the firm determination not to give up, no matter what trials and dryness one may encounter."[97]

The amount of time we spend silently listening to God will reveal the secrets of our heart. Do we really want to hear His voice so that we might do His will?

Oftentimes in spiritual direction a person will complain about their experience of God's absence in their prayer. My first question

[97] CCC 2710.

before trying to discern whether the dryness is part of God's purification is to ask whether they are being faithful to their daily time of prayer. If the response is "pretty faithful," it is not the right answer. "Pretty faithful" is not faithful. If you told your spouse that you were "pretty faithful," I am sure that wouldn't cut it.

In our fidelity to prayer, it is important to promise only what we are able to faithfully fulfill. If it is beyond your ability to commit to a holy hour every day, commit to a holy half hour. If that seems too much, start with fifteen minutes. It is important to commit to something each and every day and remain faithful to it.

On this point, there is a scene in one of the old *Pink Panther* movies that I find most applicable. Peter Sellers plays the part of Inspector Clouseau. In his desire to be at the top of his defensive skills, Clouseau would have his assistant, Cato, attack him when he least expected it. As I remember it, there was an instance in which Clouseau was about to enter a room and warned the person waiting outside that there might be a commotion when the door closed. He advised them that under no circumstances should they open the door. When Cato attacked and had the upper hand, Clouseau was quick to send out this plea, "open the door!"

When you finally carve out those fifteen minutes in your prayer time to "be still," don't open the door. No matter how hard it might seem to remain still and silent, don't open the door. Be faithful.

Fruitful: Our relationship with God can never be about just God and me.

When Jesus was asked what the greatest commandment was, He gave two: "You shall love the Lord, your God, with all your heart, with all your soul, and with all your mind. This is the greatest and the first commandment. The second is like it: You shall love your neighbor as yourself" (Matt. 22:37–39).

In Christ, there is no separation between love of God and love of neighbor. To receive His gift of contemplation, that separation cannot exist in us.

Contemplative prayer will not come to the hard of heart. God loves our enemies and has taught us to do the same (Matt. 5:44). This doesn't mean I need to have warm, fuzzy feelings toward my enemies. There were no warm, fuzzy feelings on the Cross. To love our enemy means that we never cease to hope for what is best for them. Jesus' prayer on the Cross was, "Father, forgive them, they know not what they do" (Luke 23:34). He never stopped hoping for what was best for them. In short, we cannot hold onto a grudge and hope to enter into the rest of God. Contemplative prayer is fruitful.

Free. Total. Faithful. Fruitful. When these four characteristics are manifest in our time of prayer, the kiss of contemplation will not be long off. These are the marks of a pure heart that will be led into the rest of God.

Conclusion of Part One

Part one of this book has served to prepare us for the journey of being led into the rest of God by setting our hearts on the purity that will enable us to see God as clearly as did St. Teresa of Ávila and St. John of the Cross. As mentioned in the introduction, we have now been guided through those first two possible obstacles.

The Scholastic terms upon which St. John and St. Teresa have built have been parsed out.

We now have an appreciation for the senses and the spirit, the higher part of the soul and the lower part of the soul, the active purifications and the passive purifications. The passive purifications will be described in more detail in part two.

The specific understanding St. John has of contemplative prayer is now one we would find agreeable.

Part two of this book will mark for us the ordinary path to holiness as found in their writings. What will follow is a step-by-step, chapter-by-chapter walk through of *The Interior Castle* and *The Dark Night.*

Part two will begin with the first four dwelling places of *The Interior Castle,* then turn to the first book of *The Dark Night,* and finally end with the fifth dwelling.

There is a part three that could continue with the sixth and seventh dwelling and conclude with the second book of *The Dark Night.* Perhaps one day, that too will be in your hands.

This is the order that will best accompany our experience. It will also serve to blend St. Teresa's colorful description of the "purified experience of God" with the starker description St. John gives of the "experience of God's purification."

The two work well together in helping overcome that third possible obstacle mentioned in the introduction.

***St. John's stark focus on the path of purification in* The Dark Night *is better appreciated by integrating it with* The Interior Castle.**

In my desire for these two great Doctors to speak with you directly, they will be quoted extensively. When the quote is made within the chapter being covered, no footnote will be made. The translated works from which we will quote are: St. John of the Cross, *The Dark Night,* in *The Collected Works of St. John of the Cross* (Washington, D.C., ICS, 1973) and St. Teresa of Ávila, *The Interior Castle,* in *The Collected Works of St. Teresa of Ávila, Volume Two* (Washington, D.C., ICS, 1980). A word of gratitude to ICS for granting permission to quote so extensively from these works.

With our feet now pointed in the right direction, let us allow St. John of the Cross and St. Teresa of Ávila to mark for us the path by which they were led to enter into His rest.

Part Two

Passive Purification of the Senses

Chapter 4

The Interior Castle:

The First Dwelling Place

The Beauty and Dignity of Our Souls

The Interior Castle is St. Teresa's response to the rather casual practice of prayer into which she saw her religious community falling. There is a human tendency in every age to be much more concerned with our body than our soul. Apparently, some nuns in her convent were becoming very conscientious about their physical appearance, arranging their veils in an attractive manner and even wearing jewelry. In our earthly search for things to surround the body, we often remain blind to "the precious things that are found right within our very soul." The Interior Castle is an effort to remind the reader of the "favors God is happy to grant souls and the differences between these favors." St. Teresa is well aware of the skepticism some might have in regard to what she is about to share of these favors. She warns the reader that "whoever does not believe in these favors will have no experience of them. God doesn't like us to put a limit on His works." There is also no set course by which these favors of God are received. God is free to "reveal His grandeurs to whomever He wants and sometimes does so merely to show forth His glory."

In describing the soul as an *interior castle,* St. Teresa makes it clear that "one doesn't have to enter it since it is within oneself." There is, however, "a great difference in the ways one may be inside this castle."

The Outer Courtyard

"Many souls are in the *outer courtyard.*" This is "where the guards stay — and don't care at all about entering the castle." They have no idea who dwells within the castle, how many rooms it has, or the precious things that these rooms contain. These are souls that do not pray.

She likens a soul that does not practice prayer to a person with a paralyzed or crippled body, "Even though they have hands and feet, they cannot give orders to these hands and feet." In the same manner, the soul that does not pray will not experience the beauty of the castle within.

Prayer is the Key

"The door of entry to this castle is prayer and reflection." Knowing her own community's current practice of prayer, St. Teresa is careful to clearly establish what she means by prayer. "A prayer in which a person is not aware of whom he is speaking to, what he is asking, who it is that is doing the asking and of whom, I do not call prayer however much the lips move." "Anyone in the habit of speaking before God's majesty as though he were speaking to a slave, without being careful to see how he is speaking, but saying whatever comes to his head and whatever he has learned from saying at other times, in my opinion is not praying."

In coming before Our Lord, it is important to take into consideration *whom* it is that we have this privileged opportunity to speak with.

Imagine, if we were given the chance to have a fifteen-minute audience with the pope, how carefully we might prepare for that moment. All the more should we take care how we enter our time of prayer, since it is with God that we are preparing to meet!

St. Teresa's comments reinforce the truth that prayer is intended to be an opening of our heart. Sometimes what is opened to God reveals how far we are from truly knowing Him. How tempting it is to speak to God as if He were some type of a slave — telling God what He should do. I tell God to take away my pain, to restore my loved ones to the Church, and to give favorable weather. When God doesn't answer my prayers in the way that I think He should, I can sometimes angrily reprove Him like some type of slave. *I spoke, God; did you not hear me?*

It was once related in the course of a retreat that it was the practice of one of these good sisters to sometimes pick up a statue of Jesus and start shaking it when she was frustrated in prayer. She could tell by my expression that I was shocked, to which she commented, "Well, that is just how wives sometimes speak to their spouse."

Jesus is not that kind of a spouse. He may allow it to happen for the time being, but it is something from which we will need to be purified.

A more telling description of truly praying to God is portrayed in the movie *Shadowlands*. This movie depicts the life of C. S. Lewis, in particular, the struggle he encountered with his wife's terminal diagnosis of cancer. In the midst of that trial, his pastor assured him that God was hearing his prayers, to which he replied, "I don't pray to change God; I pray to change me."

Here is someone who realized to whom he was speaking, what he was asking, and who it was that was doing the speaking.

The Darkness of Mortal Sin in the Soul

In the outer courtyard, a soul is still in the grip of mortal sin. Teresa describes the horror of mortal sin, "There is no darker darkness, nor anything more obscure and black, than to fall into mortal sin. For the intention of anyone who commits a mortal sin is not to please God, but the devil. The devil is darkness itself, and the poor soul who serves him becomes darkness."

Even so, "the light remains. Nothing can take away the beauty of God in the soul." She likens a soul in mortal sin to "a black cloth being placed over a crystal that is in the sun." Although the sun continues to shine, "its brilliance will no longer have an effect on the crystal."

Here she is likely drawing upon the distinction between *habitual grace* and *actual grace*. Habitual grace consists of the good habits we form in maintaining a permanent disposition to live and act in a manner faithful to God's call. In mortal sin, a break is made away from habitual grace. A black cloth is thrown over our soul. Even so, the light remains. The grace of God's actual presence remains in the soul. This *actual grace* keeps intervening for our conversion.[98] It is the presence of actual grace in the soul that leads Teresa to share the observation made by "a spiritual man who once stated he was not so surprised at things done by a person in mortal sin as to what was not done." Very true! Once that black cloth is thrown over the crystal of our soul, the grave possibilities of our dark actions are without limit. There is something that remains in us to intervene from making even worse decisions. We call that something, *actual grace*.

Teresa then identifies two blessings God gives us to help protect our soul from mortal sin:

1) Intense fear of offending Him

2) A mirror of humility

She relates that the time spent reading her writings "will not be lost if we are left with these two blessings." Indeed, the time will not be

98 *CCC* 2000.

lost if it gets us into the good habit of praying. It is in prayer that these two blessings grow and bear good fruit. Prayer is the habit through which the habitual graces more readily flow.

Prayer is More than Just Our Activity

To encourage us to become more consistent in this habit of prayer, Teresa entices us by recognizing that "we always hear about what a good thing prayer is; our constitutions [their Carmelite religious community rule of life] oblige us to spend many hours in prayer. Yet only what we ourselves can do in prayer is explained to us; little is explained about what the Lord does in a soul, I mean about the supernatural."

Now that should spark our interest! How often do we really consider what God is doing in our prayer? Too often, it is only about our activity.

The Image of a Castle

With our interest now piqued in the activity of God within our soul, Teresa wastes no time unfolding her image of a castle. She never discloses how the descriptions of these dwelling places are based on her own experience. Yet such clarity in writing would be impossible without an actual experience.

She is clear in explaining how the dwelling places in the castle are not to be thought of as if they "follow in file one after the other." They all surround the center room or "royal chamber where the King stays." It is a castle, not a corridor. She likely foresaw that it might be tempting to use her writings as some type of measuring device for how advanced in holiness the reader might be. That is the inherent danger of the writings of these great mystics. We might like to know what dwelling place or night we are in to somehow establish whether we are making progress in our spiritual life. This would not be utilizing the aforementioned mirror of humility very well.

To the soul being purified, these writings will give them hope that they haven't lost their way. They will help authenticate that what they are experiencing is of God. It will come as a great relief to know that they haven't succumbed to spiritual sloth by giving into their deep inclination to "enter into His rest" during the time they were accustomed to meditating.

This will be further dealt with in the fourth dwelling. To enter into the experience of that dwelling "it is very important for any soul that practices prayer — whether little or much — not to hold itself back and stay in one corner." The sun must shine in all rooms. Teresa encourages us not to stay in one room too long, unless it is the *room of self-knowledge.*

Teresa describes the room of self-knowledge as being present in every dwelling. In this room, we are able to see ourselves as God sees us. This enables us to grow in the humility necessary to consent to God's efforts to purify our heart.

A spiritual director of mine once defined holiness as "standing in the fire of self-knowledge and letting it burn." We don't normally like to spend much time in that room. This is why Teresa emphasizes, "How necessary this room is — even for those whom the Lord has brought into the very dwelling where He abides." Humility is "like the bee making honey in the beehive; it is always at work. Without it, everything goes wrong."

In each of Teresa's dwelling places, she makes an effort to stress three particular points:

1) Humble self-knowledge

2) The enemy

3) The battle

Humble Self-knowledge

The best way to grow in humility is by keeping our focus on God. "By gazing at His grandeur, we get in touch with our own lowliness; by looking at His purity, we shall see our own filth; by pondering His humility, we shall see how far we are from being humble." In striving to keep our focus on God, we will grow in self-knowledge without losing courage. To remain fixed on our earthly misery will keep us in "the mud of fears." "The fears come from not understanding ourselves completely."

It may sound strange to hear, but we really do struggle to see ourselves for who we truly are. God must show us what He sees. What He shows is always seen through the eyes of love. In His sight, I remain good, even when what I am doing is downright evil.

Catherine Doherty makes a similar point in her book *Poustinia* as she distinguishes between *introspection* and *interiorization*: "It is possible to be *introspective* in the wrong way, and this leads to worrying. *Interiorization* is God coming to you: *introspection* is yourself looking at all those idols that you should be putting [offering to the Lord] on the altar. You spend hours looking at these things when they really should simply be thrown out. *Introspection* leads you to yourself because it starts with yourself and ends with yourself. *Interiorization*, on the other hand, starts with God and ends with God. As *interiorization* increases, worrying decreases."[99]

St. Teresa teaches that it is by setting our eyes on Christ and His saints that "we shall learn true humility. The intellect will be enhanced and self-knowledge will not make one base and cowardly." "For even though this is the first dwelling place, it is very rich and so precious that if the soul slips away from the vermin within it, nothing

[99] Catherine Doherty, *Poustinia* (Combermere, ON: Madonna House, 1993, 2000), 114.

will be left to do but advance." The enemy, however, is not going to allow this to happen without a fight. Both God and the devil are going to show us our sinfulness. The devil does so to discourage and condemn us. God shows us our sins so that we can humbly repent and be saved. To be saved, we must keep our focus on Him. He alone is our only Savior.

At this point, it might prove helpful to introduce a brief way to discern spirits. There are four main spirits that need to be continually discerned. Each can be represented by an *A* word.

1) "Advocate" — the Spirit of God — who always argues for me (1 John 2:1).

2) "Accuser" — the spirit of evil — who accuses me day and night (Rev. 12:10).

3) "Amnesia" and "Anesthesia" — the spirit of the world — who tries to make me forget who I am and numb me to reality.

4) "Ass" — the spirit of self — who is simply stubborn in doing things his own way. (Realizing that the title of *spirit of self* might cause some scandal or shock, please take into consideration that it is used in light of St. Francis of Assisi, who referred to his body as "Brother Ass" — the donkey type, which proves to be stubborn.)

It is important to discern what spirit is buzzing in my brain, for they are dealt with in different fashions:

- ✠ The Advocate reveals things to set me free: I am free to consent to what He shows me.

- ✠ The Accuser reveals things to condemn me: this condemnation I must reject.
- ✠ Amnesia and Anesthesia want me to forget who I am and lose sight of the purpose of my being in this world: I must awaken it.
- ✠ The Ass stubbornly desires to do its own will: It must be disciplined to do the "will of the one who sent me" (John 5:30).

The Enemy

St. Teresa's dealings with the enemy are not very extensive in the first dwelling. Souls in this dwelling are often not convinced that the devil really exists. Concealment is among his greatest evil feats. How can we resist someone we are not sure is really there?

There is a story of interest on this point: It has been told that the devil was tied up for the past one hundred years. Upon his release, he was eager to ask his demons what the greatest sin of the past century was. He made a number of valid guesses: sexual immorality, consumerism, war, and abortion. The demons gleefully reported much success in each and every category. The greatest sin, however, could not really be told outright. To fully appreciate the greatest sin, it must be seen, so they brought him to the local cathedral, a place he knew well. He would remember with disgust how one hundred years ago, four priests would enter from the sacristy every Saturday afternoon at 3:00 p.m. to take their place in a confessional, each with a long line of waiting penitents. The demons brought him there at that precise time. When the bell struck 3:00 p.m. that Saturday afternoon, only one tired old priest came out of the sacristy, and to the confessional he entered, not a single soul stood in line. The evil one could barely contain his joy, to which the demons added, "It is even better than you think. Some do not even think there is such a thing as sin, and no one seems to be preaching about it." They then eagerly awaited their orders for what to do next and were firmly instructed, "Do nothing! If they don't think we exist, we win."

The Battle

As St. Teresa explains, "Terrible are the wiles and deceits used by the devil so that souls may not know themselves or understand their own paths." His great evil desire is for us to remain deceived about who he is, and who we really are. "The devil always has such a bad intention, so he must have in each room many legions of demons to fight off souls when they try to go from one room to the other. Since the soul doesn't know this, the devil plays tricks on it in a thousand ways."

The evil one is "not as successful with those who have advanced closer to where the King dwells." In these first rooms, souls are "still absorbed in the world." The spirit of the world numbs them to the reality of what lies beyond their desires for "pleasure, vanities, honors and pretenses." "Their vassals (senses and faculties) don't have the strength God gave our human nature in the beginning. And these souls are easily conquered."

Sometimes they are so conquered that they do not even recognize the battle they should be engaged in. Dom Augustin Guillerand, a Carthusian, observes: "Life is a battle, a battle between God and the spirit of evil. When a soul ceases to fight, it may be counted as hopelessly lost. And a soul that does not pray is one that has given in without a struggle. It possesses a kind of peace, but it is the peace of an occupied territory, conquered by the invader and resigned to his domination."[100]

[100] Dom Augustin Guillerand, *The Prayer of the Presence of God* (Manchester, NH: Sophia Institute Press, 2005), 19.

The great danger in this first dwelling is that the enemy is not recognized and the battle is not engaged in. Some souls will go so far as to insist that they are at peace with where they are, but it is the peace of an occupied territory. It is not the peace of Christ. "Jesus' peace is the result of a constant battle against evil."[101] If we are not on the devil's radar, we are most certainly in his grasp.

In this first dwelling, the danger lies in not seeing evil for what it is and failing to take up arms against our enemy. Teresa encourages souls in this first dwelling to "approach His Majesty as often as possible," to "take His Blessed Mother and His saints as intercessors so that they might fight for them and help them to humbly know themselves." For, "hardly any of the light coming from the King's royal chamber is able to reach this first dwelling." It is not as dark as one in mortal sin; nevertheless, it is so dark that the soul cannot see the light.

"The darkness is not caused by some flaw in the room." It is rather that the soul still allows so many bad things to enter that keep it unaware of the light. They continue to watch movies and television programs that fill their memories with sinful images. They allow their intellect to be filled with anxiety through what they read and listen to. They do not avoid those conversations in which they will eventually consent to gossip and slander.

The soul is still "so involved in worldly things and absorbed with its possessions, honor, or business affairs" that even though it might want to see and enjoy the beauty of God, these things do not allow it. "It is as if a person were to enter a place where the sun is shining but be hardly able to open his eyes because of the mud in them." They feel incapable of being set free from so many impediments. They simply refuse to deny themselves of what the spirit of the world insists is needed to be happy. To enter the second dwelling, "it is

[101] Benedict XVI, Angelus (August 19, 2007).

important that one strive to give up unnecessary things and business affairs. Each one is to do this in conformity with his state in life."

In every dwelling it is important to be on our guard against this numbing spirit of the world. Many persons to whom God has granted favors have fallen back into misery through their own fault. "There are few dwelling places in this castle in which the devil does not wage battle." "He enters little by little, and we don't recognize him until he's done the harm." That is why we refer to his tactics as the *insidious snares of the devil*: insidious, for they look harmless. The examples are quite literally *legion*. Teresa gives a few examples for her sisters' consideration:

Obedience: Let us say that the devil gives a sister impulses toward penance, "for it seems to her that she has no rest except when she is tormenting herself. This may be a good beginning, but if the prioress has ordered that no penance be done without permission, [while on the other hand] the devil makes the Sister think that in a practice so good, one can be rightly daring. If she secretly gives herself up to such a penitential life that she loses her health and doesn't even observe what the rule commands, you can see clearly where all this good will end."

Perfection: Another sister is imbued by the devil with a great zeal for perfection. "such zeal is in itself good. It could follow that every little fault the other Sisters commit will seem to her a serious breach; and she is careful to observe whether they commit them, and then informs the prioress. It could even happen at times that she doesn't even see her own faults because of her intense zeal of the religious observance. Since the other Sisters don't understand what's going on within her and see all this concern, they might not accept her zeal so well."

Teresa observes that what the devil is aiming at is no small thing: "The cooling of charity and love the Sisters should have for one another." This could cause serious harm. For true perfection consists in love of God and neighbor. The way he cools that charity begins through seemingly harmless moments of disobedience for the sake of penance and of judging in the striving for perfection: *insidious* snares indeed.

Chapter 5

The Interior Castle:

The Second Dwelling Place

Away from Mortal Sin, but Lacking Determination

In the rooms of this second dwelling, one has begun to practice the good habit of prayer and is coming to understand "how important it is to not stay in the first dwelling." We begin to see more clearly the reality of sin, the enemy, and the battle, but not so clear as to completely avoid the near occasions of sin. We still lack true "determination to remain in this second stage without turning back." These rooms involve much more effort than the first, and they prove to be quite dangerous. Dangerous, because the decision to return to the mortal sin of the first dwelling is now a more informed one. In the first dwelling Teresa likens us to deaf-mutes, who neither hear God nor speak of God. In this second dwelling His voice is being heard, even though our response often remains mute.

We have begun to hear the Word of God "through the words being spoken by other good people, through sermons, or through what is read in good books." We also begin to listen to Him "through our illnesses and trials, and through the truth He teaches during those brief moments we spend in prayer." "Regardless of how lukewarm these moments in prayer may be, God esteems them highly."

Our Lord is very patient with the soul. He is delighted that we are making the effort to listen to Him. He knows that we may not respond immediately to what we hear. What is important is that we persevere in trying to listen and obey what we hear.

The danger of this dwelling begins to dissipate as the soul comes to recognize more clearly what it looks like in the state of mortal sin. This instills within us a stronger desire to more soberly identify the insidious snares of the devil and engage in the battle against them.

The Enemy

Since we are no longer deaf-mutes, the devil is able to strike "in a way the soul cannot fail to hear." The devil tries to lure us into regarding "worldly things and temporal pleasures of the present as though eternal." The evil one brings to mind the esteem one has in the world, one's friends and relatives, one's health (especially in light of losing it through penitential acts) and a thousand other obstacles. "O Jesus, what an uproar the devils instigate here! And the afflictions of the poor soul: it doesn't know whether to continue or to return to the first room."

The Battle

The soul now finds itself in a battle between Heaven and earth. A person in this struggle once commented: "God and the devil decided to have a war in my head." Our *reason* begins to complain that our practice of self-denial has mistakenly undermined the value of the things of this world. Our *faith* answers back with the truth of where our real fulfillment is found. The *memory* recalls where all these worldly things are going to end — death. The *will* then becomes inclined to respond with love to the One whose love never fails.

The *intellect* helps us realize we could not have found a better friend than Jesus and recognizes that "the joys the devil offers are filled with trials, cares and contradictions." The *intellect* tells our soul that outside this castle there is neither peace nor security, so we should avoid going about to strange houses, especially since our own house is so filled with blessings. If the devil realizes that a soul has "all it needs in its temperament and habits to advance far, he will gather all of hell together to make the soul go back outside" of this dwelling and into the outer courtyard.

Humble Self-knowledge

Souls in this stage often see themselves as being further advanced in the spiritual life than they actually are. The battle to tear oneself away from the pleasures of this world is so intense that our effort can seem more heroic than it really is.

Teresa observes how amusing it is that one who still has "a thousand impediments and imperfections," whose virtues have hardly begun to grow, is not ashamed to expect the same spiritual delights in prayer that the saints experienced. She warns that one "shouldn't be thinking about consolations at this beginning stage" of prayer; it would be like setting our foundation on sand. If our aim in prayer is to receive consolations, we will "never finish being dissatisfied and tempted." "These are not the dwelling places where it rains down manna" from Heaven. Teresa reminds us that those dwellings lie further ahead. They come when our soul's only concern is to do the will of God, where we find in the manna of His will every taste we could desire.

God has made it clear that what He wants us to do is "deny ourselves and pick up our cross." In this second dwelling, our willingness to undergo exterior trials is very much conditioned by our expectation of God's interior consolations. We are quick to complain to God about crosses and dryness in prayer. In her motherly wisdom, Teresa assures us that God knows what we need, so there is no need to be advising Him about what He should give us. The whole aim of any person who is beginning to pray should not be the reception of consolations but "to prepare himself with determination and every possible effort to bring his will into conformity with God's will." For "in perfect conformity to God's will lies all our good."

We must strive to "guard ourselves against the poisonous little reptiles" that tempt us to tell God how He should act in our regard. "Sometimes God even permits these reptiles to bite us so that afterward we may know how to better guard ourselves and that He may prove whether we are grieved at having offended Him." So we should not become discouraged by falls. "For even from such falls, God will draw out good."

The Path of Perseverance

It is important for us "to consult persons with experience," who will respond with gentleness and encourage us not to give up hope. We need someone who knows how to assist us in persevering, not beat us over the head with our every fall. "Provided we don't give up, the Lord will guide everything for our benefit, even though we may not find someone to teach us." Perseverance is our duty in this second dwelling, particularly perseverance in prayer. There is "no remedy for the evil of giving up prayer than to begin again; otherwise the soul will gradually lose more each day."

Chapter 6

The Interior Castle: *The Third Dwelling Place*

A Time of Consolation for Turning to God

In the third dwelling, one is away from the road of destruction (mortal sin) and on the blessed path to salvation. For the soul who, through the mercy of God, has persevered through these tumultuous battles and entered the rooms of this third dwelling, Teresa can think of no better words than "Blessed is the man who fears the Lord" (Ps. 112:1). The fear of turning away from God has pointed their feet more firmly in the right direction. God now comforts the soul for having turned to Him.

The Enemy

In this dwelling, we recognize the enemy's presence. Teresa observes that it can seem "a great misery to live a life in which we must always walk like those whose enemies are at their doorstep." What is even more miserable is the possibility of losing our place with God. The thought of "living without God" and the fear of "losing Him forever" is "nothing else than dying often." To emphasize this point, Teresa draws upon the words of St. Thomas, who asserted his willingness to die with Jesus in order to remain with Him (John 11:16).

The Battle

We now desire to engage in the battle against the enemy. The fear of living without God or losing His favor spurs us on to take up arms. With this fear we are blessed, for there is no greater happiness than the desire to please God. In this dwelling, "they long not to offend His Majesty, even guarding themselves against venial sins; they are fond of doing penance and setting aside periods for recollection; they spend their time well, practicing works of charity toward their neighbors; and are very balanced in their use of speech and dress and in the governing of their households."

A strong desire is now experienced to enter into the final dwelling place. Teresa warns, however, "It is not enough to simply say we want it." The danger can now surface in not being patient enough to allow the King to open the door when He desires. Now that we consider ourselves His vassals (one whose life is at His service), we can assume that we should be free to enter where the pure of heart have already secured a place.

Humble Self-knowledge

In this dwelling, the truth remains hidden that we have turned to God more for our own sake than for Him. We enjoy being in this dwelling because it *feels* much better than the previous dwelling places. Our spiritual life is not yet a response of pure love for God. Our heart still needs to be purified. This is not the dwelling for purification. This is a dwelling of encouragement. God first needs to strengthen our resolve to live for Him alone before He can begin to purify our hearts of what is still not set on Him.

In this dwelling it is important "to behold the lives of the saints who entered this King's chamber, and see the difference between them and us." We must avoid the temptation "to ask for what we have not deserved, nor should we even allow it to enter our minds that we have merited this favor from Him, however much we may have served Him." Let it be enough that we now desire to be God's vassals, otherwise our hearts could be set on so much "that as a result we are left with nothing."

To help us recognize that our motivation in prayer remains quite selfish, God will begin to withdraw the experience of His consolations. Teresa comments on how "anyone who makes an issue of this dryness is a little lacking in humility." Dryness in prayer should be a welcome opportunity to prove ourselves, to show in a concrete way that we are turning to God because we love Him, not just because we love how He makes us feel. "If, like the young man in the Gospel, we turn our backs and go away sad when the Lord tells us what we must do to be perfect, what do you want His Majesty to do?"

God will only give the reward of Himself in conformity with the authentic love we have for Him. This love "cannot be fabricated in our imaginations," as in meditation, "but it is proven through our deeds." Not that God needs our works; what He is looking for is our determination of will. Are our hearts truly set upon God alone? Are we now ready to be purified of all that is not purely set on Him? The answers to these questions will surface as God begins to withhold His consolations.

Teresa points out how helpful it is "to consider ourselves as useless servants," to whom the Lord is under no obligation to grant favors. Rather, since we have already received much, all the more are we indebted. We should "consider ourselves lucky to be able to repay something of what we owe Him for His service toward us." God has done "nothing else but serve us all the time He lived in this world, and yet we ask Him again for favors and gifts."

These are important points for our reflection that will help us appreciate what St. John of the Cross is about to tell us through his writing of *The Dark Night*. The process through which God will draw us from the third dwelling to the fourth dwelling is described well in *The Dark Night*. This is where the *passive purifications* begin. The experience of dryness in prayer is the work of God's hand, intended to lead us to humility. The enemy will try to get us disturbed by it. He knows that in this third dwelling, true humility often proves to be lacking.

In regard to prayer, Teresa wants us to realize that "consolations are given to weaker souls." In a *weaker soul*, as Teresa puts it, God continues to give consolations in prayer so that these souls don't turn away from the practice of prayer. God sees that they are not yet ready to walk the path of pure love for Him. He waits until they are ready for Him to purify their hearts of their attachment to receiving consolations for turning to Him. She observes how even *stronger souls* are unlikely to "exchange these consolations for the fortitude of those who walk in dryness." We all prove to be "fonder of consolations than we are of the cross." Teresa concludes this chapter with this wise prayer: "Test us, Lord — for You know the truth — so that we may know ourselves." The test is indeed coming.

Falling Prey to an Illusion

The consolations can be so intense in this third dwelling that we can think we have arrived at the top of the spiritual mountain. It is not uncommon for a soul who has reached this state and has lived many years in this "upright and well-ordered way" to fall prey to an illusion. It seems to them that they have become "lords of this world" by having denied themselves some of its pleasures and knowing where their true treasure is. God "will then try them in some minor matters, and they go about so disturbed and afflicted" that it is truly concerning. Teresa sadly observes that it is often "useless to try and give them advice, for since they have engaged so long in the practice of virtue they think they can teach others and that they are more than justified in feeling disturbed. She continues, "I have found neither a way of consoling nor a cure for such persons other than to show them compassion in their affliction — and indeed, compassion is felt on seeing them subject to so much misery."

They are convinced that all they suffer is for God. It is almost impossible to help them see that these disturbances are the result of an imperfection within them. It is a great temptation "to canonize these feelings in their minds and desire others to do so." Teresa cites a few examples to help us "test ourselves before the Lord tests us":

Loss of Wealth: A rich person without dependents loses wealth, "not to such an extent that he lacks necessities for himself and for the management of his household; he even has a surplus. If he should go about as worried and disturbed as he would if not even a piece of bread were left, how can our Lord ask him to leave all for Him? Here the person makes the excuse that he feels the way he does because he wants these things for the poor. I believe that God has a greater desire that such a person conform to the divine will."

Although the souls in this third dwelling have finally made a place for God in their lives, it often remains just a place. God is not yet the Master of their house. In order for Our Lord to lead us into the further dwellings of His rest, we will need to learn that "no one can serve two masters" (Matt. 6:24).

Acquiring Wealth: Teresa continues this theme in an example of a person aspiring to acquire more wealth. She admits that this is not always an impediment to spiritual growth, "but if he strives for wealth and after possessing it strives for more and more, however good the intention may be (for he should have a good intention because, as we have said, these are virtuous persons of prayer), he need have no fear of ascending to the dwelling places closest to the King."

Our King of Kings has taught us, "where your treasure is, there also will your heart be" (Matt. 6:21). In this third dwelling, we are still concerned with storing up "treasures on earth" (Matt. 6:19). Like the rich young man of the Gospel, we become sad when Jesus invites us to "sell all that you have and distribute it to the poor, and you will have a treasure in heaven. Then come, follow me" (Luke 18:22). We are not yet willing to be led "to the dwelling places closest to the King." There are still other treasures that have a stronger hold on our heart.

Loss of Honor: One more good example Teresa offers is when an "opportunity presents itself for these persons to be despised or to lose a little honor." Even though these same souls may have long considered Our Lord's sufferings and even desired to share in His sufferings, they can become greatly disturbed when being misunderstood or mistreated by others. They often claim that their grief is due to the faults of others who aren't able to see things as spiritually as they do. They fail to see the great favor Our Lord is granting them to grow in virtue and to show in a concrete way that they are worthy of being treated in the same manner as the Master.

Humility to the Rescue

In all of the aforementioned examples, and in every one that might be cited, it is humility that comes to the rescue. "Humility is the ointment for our wounds" of pride. If we have humility, "even though there may be a time of delay, the surgeon, who is our Lord, will come to heal us." "With humility present, this stage is a most excellent one. If humility is lacking, we will remain here our whole life."

Although we are now on the road to salvation, we have yet to be led into His rest. It requires humility to allow God to show us the way into the further dwelling places. We can be tempted to think we know the right path and how to walk on it when the Lord might want to take us there by a shortcut. It is a "laborious and burdensome" task to think that we need to figure out the way to holiness. If we remain in this third dwelling it will be with "a thousand afflictions and miseries." When our reason remains too much in control, love has not yet reached the fever pitch it needs to be at to learn that His "ways are not our ways" (see Isa. 55:8).

The "Little Way" Is No Easier

St. Teresa of Ávila and St. John of the Cross are about to reveal what it is that keeps us from being led into intimacy with God, the union with Him we claim to desire. As mentioned in the introduction, some claim their writings are too much for the average person to understand. And when we begin to understand them, it can be hard to accept what they have to say. Even St. Thérèse of Lisieux claimed to find it a bit dizzying to look at the "rough stairway of perfection" as laid out by St. John of the Cross in book two of his *Dark Night*. Thérèse claimed to find a "little way," "an elevator which would raise me to Jesus, for I am too small to climb the rough stairway of perfection."[102]

Thérèse was being a bit playful, for her *little way* was no small doing. She knew that: "Sanctity does not consist in this or that practice; it consists in a disposition of heart which makes us humble and little in the arms of God, conscious of our weakness, and confident to the point of audacity in the goodness of our Father."[103]

St. Thérèse was beautifully aware of her weaknesses and realized her need to "bear with myself such as I am with all my imperfections."[104] Thérèse was charmingly disarming, as she claimed to be an "obscure grain of sand" in the midst of the

[102] St. Thérèse of Lisieux, *Story of a Soul*, 207.

[103] St. Thérèse of Lisieux, *Her Last Converations*, 129.

[104] St. Thérèse of Lisieux, *Story of a Soul*, 207.

"mountain whose summit is lost in the clouds."[105] The mountain she is referring to is the holy mother and holy father of her Discalced Carmelite Order: St. Teresa of Ávila and St. John of the Cross. We all know the truth that Thérèse was no small giant when it comes to the path of purification. Her little way was to honestly acknowledge each and every imperfection and give it straight to God for Him to purify. This little way is simple, but it is not easy. Most of us need God to give us a little more help in this process of purification. Thérèse was obviously no stranger to His purifying hand as she comments, "Our holy Mother St. Teresa" had "no fears of revealing the secrets of the King in order that they might make Him more loved and known by souls."[106] Thérèse may have held that dark purifying path very close to her pure heart, as the "secrets of the King," to see Him.

There is something fresh about St. Thérèse, who at the time of her writing is giving every weakness and impurity straight to God. We might be drawn to run to "The Little Flower" in our flight from the "rough stairway of perfection." There is, of course, no escaping the one path of discipleship, to "deny yourself, pick up your cross, and follow me." When Thérèse assures us that "the Lord has said: Tell the just man ALL is well" (see Isa. 3:10), she quickly follows with "Yes, all is well when one seeks only the will of Jesus."[107] This should sound familiar. Thérèse merely echoes the wisdom of her holy mother and holy father, St. Teresa of Ávila and St. John of the Cross.

St. Thérèse can be counted among those from whom St. Teresa encourages us to seek counsel. We all need someone who will help us see more clearly the will of God, someone whose own example can encourage us. For "through the flight of these others we also will

[105] Ibid.
[106] Ibid.
[107] Ibid.

make bold to fly, as do the bird's fledglings when they are taught; for even though they do not begin to soar immediately, little-by-little they imitate the parent."

We are all in need of good spiritual parents. We benefit so much from the guidance of those who are "free from the illusion about the things of this world" and are intent on protecting us from doing our own will. We are wise in seeking counsel from someone who can show us the way to the Father and help us see when we are doing our own will. It will help us to look at someone we see doing things with ease that we ourselves might think impossible. Sometimes God will grace us with a spiritual mother or father who is in the flesh. We will also find great counsel from those holy spiritual mothers and fathers of the Faith who have already flown where we one day hope to spread our wings. The beauty of our communion with the saints is that we can all find someone who truly speaks to our soul. I myself have found few better spiritual directors than St. Teresa of Ávila, St. Thérèse of Lisieux, and St. John of the Cross.

Chapter 7

The Interior Castle:

The Fourth Dwelling Place

"Where the Supernatural Experience Begins"

These are the dwellings in which the activity of God becomes more apparent in our time of prayer. This is "where the supernatural experience begins." "Since these dwelling places are closer to where the King is, their beauty is great." What we experience here is "so delicate that the intellect is incapable of finding words to explain them." As St. Paul observed: "What eye has not seen, and ear has not heard, and what has not entered the human heart, what God has prepared for those who love him" (1 Cor. 2:9).

Normally one must have lived in the other dwelling places for a long time to reach these, but "the Lord gives when He desires, as He desires, and to whom He desires. Since these blessings belong to Him, He does no injustice to anyone" in giving or withholding these favors.

It is critical to bear in mind that we can never merit such precious gifts. The experience of God's activity in our soul can only happen through His mercy. St. Teresa's careful description of these dwellings will help us appreciate the gifts God desires to give and hopefully encourage us to be better disposed to receiving them. The danger in describing these favors in a hierarchical fashion is that they might be used as a type of spiritual progress chart. Her description of God's activity in prayer is not intended to be used as a holiness litmus test. A castle in which we make our dwelling with God is being described, not a corridor to march down.

There was a sister I was directing who was very interested, almost obsessed, about determining what dwelling she was in. All the while she complained that she felt like she was under the kitchen sink with Jesus. To which I observed, "If you are under the kitchen sink with Jesus, stay there with Him! Don't go searching for a room in which He is not yet leading you to enter."

The dwellings, in fact, are not actual places of existence. St. Teresa's writings are a tool for us to help authenticate our experience of God in our soul. They are meant to help us enjoy wherever we are with Jesus without spending too much time trying to figure out where we match up with the mystics. Humility is the first sign that our experience of God's activity in our soul is authentic. Humility keeps us rooted in the truth that only God can make us holy. As the Gloria reminds us: "You alone are the Holy One!" All holiness belongs to God. We could take no more credit for being made holy by God than for one who steps out of a dark room and into the sun to take credit for having the light now shine upon them.

Our Blessed Virgin Mary can help us keep this all in mind. Her holiness is very clearly the activity of God in her soul. Her receptivity to His mercy began in her Immaculate Conception. She did nothing to merit being conceived in her mother's womb without sin. It was a pure gift of God.

In the Annunciation, Mary allows God to do whatever He desires in her soul. "Let it be accomplished in me according to your word" (Luke 1:38). Our Blessed Mother's holiness is not so much about what she did in prayer, but what she allowed God to do in her soul. As she revealed to her cousin Elizabeth, "The Almighty has done great things for me" (Luke 1:49). "He has looked with favor on His lowly servant" (v. 48).

Reflecting on the holiness of our Blessed Mother brings to mind St. Teresa's words at the beginning of *The Interior Castle*: "We always hear about what a good thing prayer is; our constitutions oblige us to spend many hours in prayer. Yet only what we ourselves can do in prayer is explained to us; little is explained about what the Lord does in a soul, I mean about the supernatural."

The depth of Mary's holiness reflects how she did nothing to hinder what the Lord does in a soul. In the Annunciation, Mary gave God full access to her whole being — past, present, and future.

Past, "I have not known man" (Luke 1:34).

Present, "Behold the handmaid of the Lord" (v. 38).

Future, "Let it be done to me according to your word" (v. 38).

To pray as Mary prays, we, too, must give God full access to our lives: past, present, and future. In striving to give God full access, do not be surprised by distractions: distractions from the past, distractions of the present, and even distractions concerning the future.

Be assured that:

- ✠ God is not surprised by our past; so don't waste your time trying to hide those facts from Him;
- ✠ God is not shocked by our present distractions and impurities; He sees them before they are even on our mind;
- ✠ God is not worried about our future, so keep it in His hands;
- ✠ What has been, has been. What is, is. What will be, will be.

The best we can do with distractions we encounter, as we prepare a quiet place to welcome the desired guest of our soul, is to give them straight to God. We try to enter prayer with our distractions left at the door. If they come in with us, give them to God. Otherwise, the time we spend in prayer might be consumed by trying to chase these thoughts out the door.

It is helpful to draw a distinction between *distractions* and *excuses*.

- ✠ A *distraction* is something that keeps me from my desired goal. It is something to persevere through.
- ✠ An *excuse* gives me permission to return to what I find more immediately gratifying.

If my sincere intention is to be led into these further dwellings, then I must firmly resolve not to give up, no matter what distractions may come. The *Catechism* helps us to appreciate that "the choice of the *time and duration of the prayer* arises from a determined will, revealing the secrets of the heart. One does not undertake contemplative prayer only when one has the time: one makes time for the Lord, with the firm determination not to give up, no matter what trials and dryness one may encounter."[108]

As mentioned earlier, when we sit down to pray, all the things we had forgotten can suddenly seem to be remembered. Sometimes we can use this as an excuse to get up and do those things instead of sitting through another dry time of prayer. When our intention to wait upon the Lord is firm, we realize that if these distracting reminders are from the Lord, they will come back to us after the appointed time of prayer. The determined effort to "be still, and know that I am God" (Ps. 46:11) is the hard work of prayer. Anyone who makes light of that work has not truly put their hand to it.

[108] CCC 2710.

The Enemy

We can be sure that the enemy is going to be very busy bringing to the fore every possible distraction. He had been content to see us do all the talking and thinking in prayer, but now we are opening ourselves to the activity of God. We are trying to listen to Him. The evil one will not allow that to happen without a fierce battle.

Within the actual experience of the prayerful rest that will be described in this fourth dwelling, the evil one is not able to enter. Both Teresa and John observe how the soul is then too united to God for the enemy to dare penetrate. However, Teresa realizes that it not possible to be left in a continual state of absorption. The ferocious attacks that will surround these restful experiences in prayer actually help the soul not to lose sight of how dependent they are upon the mercy of God.

Different Types of Prayer and Their Effects

St. Teresa now begins to describe the activity of God that unfolds in our soul in this fourth dwelling. To better reflect what is being experienced, she will use the term *prayer of quiet* in place of *contemplation*. To help us understand the prayer of quiet, she contrasts it with the more common experience of meditation. Whether she intended it or not, she uses the philosophical principle of cause and effect. In this principle we first examine the effects in order to better understand the cause, like a mother who looks at the *effects* of the shattered pieces of her favorite vase lying on the floor alongside a baseball in order to determine the *cause* of how it broke. In similar fashion, Teresa will begin her examination of the difference between the prayer of quiet and meditation by first focusing on their effects of spiritual delights and consolations.

A type of flowchart for her "cause and effect" of prayer might look like this:

Cause → Effect

Meditation → Consolations

Prayer of Quiet → Spiritual Delights

Now let's examine them in detail.

Consolations vs. Spiritual Delights

"Through our own meditation and petitions to the Lord" we often experience *consolations*. The interior experience of consolation in prayer is similar to our experience of other earthly consolations. "For example, when someone suddenly inherits a great fortune; when we suddenly see a person we love very much; when we succeed in a large and important business matter and of which everyone speaks well; when you see your husband or brother or son alive after someone told you he is dead." In a similar way, these "joyful consolations in prayer have their beginning in our human nature and end in God." God still has a hand in them, for "without Him we can do nothing." It is simply that these "consolations arise from the virtuous work that we perform, and it seems that we have earned them through our own effort and are rightly consoled for having engaged in such deeds."

Spiritual delights, on the other hand, "begin in God." Even though our human nature feels and enjoys them as it does consolations, what is experienced in the soul is much different. Teresa finds it difficult to put the experience of a spiritual delight into precise words, yet she regards these few words as sufficient: "You open my docile heart" (*Cum dilatasti cor meum*) (Ps. 119:32).

"For anyone who has had much experience, these words are sufficient to see the difference between consolations and spiritual delights; for anyone who has not, more words are needed."

A further word might prove helpful here.

The consolations we often experience in prayer normally accompany a specific activity. During the prayerful recitation of the Rosary, the Stations of the Cross, or while meditating on a passage of Sacred Scripture, we may experience a consolation. Since the consolation arose from a specific devotion, it is easy to become attached to that spiritual activity in the hope of receiving a similar consolation. We can become confused in thinking that these consolations are somehow earned through our acts of prayer and devotion.

A spiritual delight, on the other hand, comes without us knowing how it happened. The one who receives it is utterly aware that it did not proceed from their own activity. It came without them knowing how it happened and is beyond what our human nature could have led us to.

> A consolation can constrict our life of prayer if we become attached to the devotions through which they come.
>
> A spiritual delight comes without us knowing how it happened and expands our heart to the deeper possibilities of God's touches.

To draw out this distinction, consider the difference between receiving a kiss from your beloved after having prepared their favorite dinner and having them kiss you completely out of the blue. The first kiss might leave you thinking you earned it; the other expands your heart to the deeper possibilities of their love.

To receive spiritual delights, St. Teresa stresses that the important thing in prayer is "not to think much, but to love much." "Do that which best stirs you to love," realizing that "love does not consist in great delight but in desiring with strong determination to please God in everything."

On the topic of thinking, she makes an important distinction between the *intellect* and the *imagination*. The *intellect* is one of the soul's faculties. The *imagination* is what goes on inside our brain. Teresa recognized in her prayer that it is possible that "the faculties of my soul were occupied and recollected in God even while my mind, on the other hand, was distracted." In other words, "all this turmoil in our head doesn't hinder prayer." There is an *interior castle* within us. Even when our imagination is filled with distractions, our intellect is still able to assist our will in making many beautiful acts of surrender, love, and trust. The soul can still be "completely taken up in its quiet, love, desires, and clear knowledge." Again, the hard work of prayer is to keep surrendering all the distractions of our imagination into the hands of Our Lord as we strive to be still before Him in our intellect.

Now comes a very telling and important observation:

> **"The pain of distraction is felt when suspension does not accompany prayer."**

What St. Teresa means by *suspension* will be unfolded further in the next chapter as she explains the *prayer of quiet*. By all outward appearances, a suspension will make it appear as if a person has fallen asleep. In the seventh stanza of his poem, "The Dark Night," St. John of the Cross describes how "He wounded my neck, suspending all of my senses." When the neck is wounded, the person nods off.

Both Teresa and John recognize the suspension of our senses as an experience that typically happens as we begin to receive the gift of contemplation. It is the activity of God drawing us into the spirit by putting our senses to sleep. Our Lord is beginning to lead us into His rest. Even though our whole being desires to follow Him, we can be tempted to fight it off through pride, especially if we are praying in community. Who wants to look like they are sleeping?

If we go there, it is not a journey to dreamland. We remain aware of what is going on around us, even though our senses are completely suspended by God. This is what happens when God touches the soul. His full embrace will put the body and its senses down for good — eternal rest! God sees that it is now safe for Him to touch our soul without doing any harm. He holds off until we begin to grow in the virtues, especially humility. If the touch came too soon, it would likely lead to spiritual pride in thinking that we somehow earned it. The soul is nowhere near the union of the seventh dwelling, where the senses and faculties are working together in restful harmony. In this fourth dwelling, it is God Himself who now binds the senses and faculties into this marvelous rest.

Entering into His rest must be the regained focus of our time in prayer — to rest in Him. The beginning of that rest must be embarked upon in a humbling way. In this suspension, we still hear what is going on around us. We might even question whether we are sleeping, which, to me, is the sure sign that you are not sleeping. Have you ever questioned whether you are sleeping while you are actually sleeping?

Furthermore, St. John of the Cross will recognize that this rest "fires the soul in a spirit of love,"[109] even though the soul seemed to be doing nothing. That is the beauty of the way God unfolds His plan of contemplation. He makes it evident from the beginning that it is now He who is at work within our soul, pouring out blessings upon His beloved while they slumber (see Ps. 127:2). *It is what God does in prayer.*

[109] St. John of the Cross, *The Dark Night*, 1.10.6

Prayer of Quiet vs. Mental Prayer

To help make the distinction between the *prayer of quiet* and *mental prayer,* St. Teresa describes the different ways in which two troughs are filled with water.

With *mental prayer,* "the water comes from far away through many aqueducts and the use of much ingenuity."

In the *prayer of quiet,* "the source of the water is right there, and the trough fills without any noise." "There is no need of any skill, nor does the building of aqueducts have to continue."

While consolations require the work of meditation, spiritual delights simply spring up from within during the prayer of quiet. The spring of spiritual delights fills the trough without any noise. It is the activity of God "welling from within up to eternal life" (John 4:14). This is why it is so important for us to learn how to "be still" during our time of prayer: "Silence, all mankind, in the presence of the Lord! for he stirs forth from his holy dwelling" (Zech. 2:17).

St. Teresa returns to the words of Psalm 119, "You open my docile heart," to describe how in these spiritual delights "heavenly water begins to rise from this spring that is deep within us, it swells and expands our whole interior being, producing ineffable blessings."

"The spiritual delight is not something that can be imagined, because however diligent our efforts, we cannot acquire it." We are unable to understand what is being given. "Here the faculties are not united (as in the seventh dwelling), but absorbed and looking on as though in wonder at what they see."

Still, "the will must in some way be united with God's will." The will must consent to this wonderful activity, consenting at the very least to the humiliation of looking like we are asleep during this time of prayer. The best way for us to test whether this is truly the prayer of quiet is from the deeds that follow afterward.

There was a sweet little sister who came up to me after this talk on the fourth dwelling to relate how she had experienced these spiritual delights. When it happened, however, the novice mistress came over to wake her up. In fact, she was so disturbed by this little sleeping nun that she did not allow her to rest that day or the next during the normal midday repose. This mistress was looking at the wrong place during her own time of prayer. She should have had her eyes on Jesus. Looking at the exterior posture of her novices during prayer is not a good way to evaluate what is happening interiorly. Pay attention to what happens afterwards. If you have a person who emerges from their time of resting in the Lord more alive than ever to do the works of mercy with great joy, then you likely have a contemplative on your hands. If, on the other hand, they arouse lazy, complaining, and uncharitable, then you have a sleeper.

The first sign St. Teresa gives for recognizing if this prayer is from God is *humility*. We will realize that we did not "deserve these favors and spiritual delights from the Lord or that you will receive them [again] in your lifetime." We will be aware that something this good cannot come from our own meager efforts. This will protect us from expecting them to happen again. God will not give spiritual delights when we are seeking them. Teresa gives the following five reasons why the path of not striving for spiritual delights is the surest way of receiving them:

1) "The initial thing necessary for such favors is to love God without self-interest."

2) It would lack humility to think something so great could be obtained by our miserable service.

3) The proper preparation for sinners to receive favors is the desire to suffer and imitate the Lord.

4) God is not obliged to give these favors.

5) We would be laboring in vain for these favors, since they are given only to whom God wills and they often come when the soul least expects it.

These observations underscore what was observed in the first chapter of the third dwelling: God will only give the reward of Himself in conformity with the authentic love we have for Him. As long as we are seeking something for ourselves or thinking we can earn these favors from God, "in vain is our earlier rising and going later to bed" (Ps. 127:2).

Prayer of Recollection

The *prayer of recollection* actually comes before the *prayer of quiet.*

In reading the writings of St. Teresa of Ávila, one of the difficulties people can experience is that her thoughts do not always flow systematically. I admit there are times when I need to put down her writings to try and organize in my mind what she is conveying. She can sometimes seem a bit scattered. We have to remember that she did not have a computer with "cut and paste" ability, but she realized various experiences that were important to explain.

So we can now add to our **Cause and Effect Prayer Flowchart** the *Prayer of Recollection* and *Our Efforts to be Recollected in Prayer.*

Cause → Effect

Our Efforts to be Recollected in Prayer → Meditation → Consolations

Prayer of Recollection → Prayer of Quiet → Spiritual Delights

The *prayer of recollection* is different than our own efforts to be quiet and still before Our Lord. In St. Teresa's wise words, "It doesn't involve being in the dark or closing the eyes." Turning off the lights and closing our eyes are our own good efforts to be *recollected in prayer*. In the *prayer of recollection,* "without first wanting to do so, one does close one's eyes and desire solitude." It is now the hand of God drawing our senses and faculties gently inward. Teresa observes that it is only God who can "absorb us" into this *prayer of recollection*. Without His guiding hand she "cannot understand how the mind can be stopped," regardless of how diligent our efforts are to be *recollected in prayer*.

There was evidently a lot of debate in St. Teresa's day about how contemplation begins. Some were contending that one could bring about contemplation by one's own efforts to meditate. Teresa remarks that meditation is the proper preparation for contemplation, but contemplation remains the activity of God.

It is what God does in prayer.

She stresses that the *prayer of recollection* is the gate through which one enters into the *prayer of quiet*; it is "the beginning through which one goes to the other." She strongly warns those who think they can bring about the *prayer of recollection* by their own efforts: "Don't think this *recollection* is acquired by the intellect striving to think about God within itself, or by the imagination imagining Him within itself. Such efforts are good and an excellent kind of *meditation* — but this is not the *prayer of recollection,* because it is something each one can do."

The *prayer of recollection* is the supernatural activity of God in our soul.

It is what God does in prayer.

St. Teresa gives the following four reasons that distinguish this type of *recollection* as very different from our own efforts to be quiet and still.

1) "In this work of the spirit, one begins to think less and has less desire to act."

2) "These interior works are all gentle and peaceful; doing something arduous would cause more harm than good."

3) "The very care used not to think of anything, will perhaps rouse the mind to think very much."

4) "What is most essential and pleasing to God is that we be mindful of His honor and glory and forget ourselves and our own profit and comfort and delight."

In our own efforts to be *recollected in prayer,* St. Teresa considers it impossible to clear our minds of every possible thought. Again, without His guiding hand she "cannot understand how the mind can be stopped." Her advice is to stop thinking about ourselves and start thinking about God; "It is good to be aware that one is in God's presence." Then, "when His Majesty desires the intellect to stop, He occupies it in another way and gives it a light so far above what we can attain that it remains absorbed." When His Majesty does come in this way, she encourages us to "not strive to understand the nature of this recollection." "Let the soul enjoy it without any endeavors other than some loving words."

She then gives advice that should be highlighted and underlined:

"One should leave the intellect go and surrender oneself into the arms of love, for His Majesty will teach the soul what it must do at that point."

In *The Living Flame of Love,* St. John of the Cross observes how few souls reach the high state of perfect union with God. Although God certainly desires all to be perfect, "He finds few vessels that will endure so lofty and sublime a work."[110] Again, the work of preparing ourselves for contemplation is not to be taken lightly.

How hard it is to "leave the intellect go and surrender oneself into the arms of love." This requires a true denial of *self.*

St. John of the Cross will observe that although many souls "desire to advance and persistently beseech God to bring them to this state of perfection, when God wills to conduct them through the initial trials and mortifications, as is necessary, they are unwilling to suffer them, and they shun them, flee from the narrow road of life, and seek the broad road of their own consolation, which is that of their own perdition; thus they do not allow God to begin to grant their petition."[111]

The rich young man we spoke of earlier did not allow Jesus to grant his petition. When Jesus told him what he must do "to inherit eternal life" (Mark 10:17), "he went away sad, for he had many possessions" (v. 22). Our Lord then gave us all this stark warning: "How hard it is for those who have wealth to enter the kingdom of God!" (v. 23).

Jesus was very clear: "If you wish to be perfect, go, sell what you have and give to the poor, and you will have treasure in heaven" (Matt. 19:21). We must be ready to depart from the more secure

[110] St. John of the Cross, *The Collected Works of St. John of the Cross, The Living Flame of Love,* stanza 2, par. 27.

[111] Ibid.

path of consolations in order for the Lord to purify our hearts to see Him in the fashion St. John and St. Teresa are going to describe for us. To be led into these deeper dwellings, we must be purified of each and every attachment that would hinder us from swimming "in the unctions [oils of anointing] of God."[112]

It is getting ahead of ourselves to speak of the unctions of God while still examining the fourth dwelling. In speaking of them now, it is with the hope that we might be inspired with a greater desire to put into practice the wisdom Teresa imparts in this dwelling and that John is about to share in his work of *The Dark Night*. By following Teresa's advice to "leave the intellect go and surrender oneself into the arms of love," we will be better prepared to swim in these unctions of God. For John will observe how the devil "makes the soul lose abundant riches by alluring it with a little bait — as one would allure a fish — out of simple waters of the spirit, where it was engulfed and swallowed up in God without finding any bottom or foothold. And by this bait he provides it with a prop and drags it ashore so that it might find the ground and go on foot with great effort, rather than swim in the unctions of God."[113]

If we don't "leave the intellect go and surrender oneself into the arms of love," we will be easily drawn out of the solitude and recollection of these deep waters of prayer. The devil will bait us into seriously considering that it must be better for us to do something in this time of prayer rather than to just sit in quiet, resting in God.[114]

We may recall in our childhood being told by our parents, "Don't just sit there, do something." Our Heavenly Father now looks at us in prayer with love and invites us to "Don't just do something, sit there."

[112] Ibid., 3.64.

[113] Ibid.

[114] Ibid., 3.63.

Benefits

The benefits of surrendering the intellect cannot be overemphasized as we begin in *The Dark Night* to examine in fine detail the purifying path by which this surrender will take place. Why would anyone want to "leave the intellect go and surrender oneself into the arms of love" when the "arms of love" don't seem to encompass the same type of pleasures enjoyed in the imagination through meditation? It requires great confidence in God to allow our experience in prayer to be expanded beyond what "eye can see and ear can hear" (see 1 Cor. 2:9). The expansion spoken of in the *prayer of quiet* will strengthen our trust in the Good Shepherd who knows the path that brings us beyond our fears and into His rest (see Ps. 23).

St. Teresa now spells out some of these benefits in detail:

- ✠ The fear of Hell is replaced with a fear of offending God.
- ✠ The fear of "doing penance and losing its health" disappears as we now regard all things as possible in God.
- ✠ The fear of trials is now tempered as we become aware that what we suffer is suffered for the Lord.
- ✠ We are now more patient in suffering and desire to do all things for God, even to suffer for Him.
- ✠ We recognize more clearly the emptiness of worldly delights and, little by little, begin to withdraw from them.
- ✠ In sum, there is an improvement in all the virtues.

Perseverance, the Enemy, and the Battle

Even though in this dwelling the soul is now more committed than ever to allow Our Lord to lead it on this spiritual journey, St. Teresa warns that the soul is not yet grown; "It is like a suckling child." "If it turns away from its mother's breast, what can be expected for it but death? Great care must be taken to not offend God."

> I advise them so strongly not to place themselves in the occasions of sin because the devil tries much harder for a soul of this kind than for very many to whom the Lord does not grant these favors. For such a soul can do a great deal of harm to the devil by getting others to follow it, and could be of great benefit to God's Church. And even though the devil may have no other reason than to see who it is to whom His Majesty shows particular love, that's sufficient for him to wear himself out trying to lead the soul to perdition.

The enemy cannot see what is happening during this time of prayer. He is infuriated by what this seemingly useless time in prayer is doing for this soul. He wages a direct war against the soul outside of its time of prayer. "These souls suffer much combat, and if they go astray, they stray more than do others."

The sad truth is that good holy souls can sometimes stray far from the Faith. At this stage, the combat of faith is not about a particular article of faith. As Pope Benedict XVI reflected in his *Introduction to Christianity*, "What is at stake is the whole structure; it is a question of all or nothing."[115]

In this dwelling it is becoming clear that I either surrender everything to God, placing my full trust in His will, or I keep clinging to my own will in seeking the comforts of this world.

[115] Benedict XVI, *Introduction to Christianity*, 43.

Introduction to *The Dark Night*

Preliminary Remarks on *The Dark Night*

All the pieces are now in place for us to appreciate the wisdom of St. John of the Cross in *The Dark Night.*

- ✠ The Scholastic terms he uses have been parsed out.
- ✠ The understanding he has of contemplative prayer is one that we now share.
- ✠ The rather stark description he will relate of the experience of God's purification has been buffered by St. Teresa's more colorful description of the purified experience of God.

Before we proceed to a step-by-step analysis of his text, you might enjoy (and identify with) these few preliminary remarks made in light of comments that have surfaced during the retreats and classes I have given on this material.

The Dark Night as God's Gift

On a ride from the airport to a Missionary of Charity convent in Albania, one of the sisters inquired about the topic of the retreat. When I replied, "*The Dark Night,*" she groaned the complaint that what she needed was light! So, this first remark is the simple assurance that *the dark night* is indeed a gift of God's light.

The dark night is an often-misunderstood gift of God. The dark night comes when His light begins to shine upon my soul to purify my heart at a level I cannot do on my own. Purity of heart is best understood as a gift from God. The words of Psalm 51 teach us to pray, "A pure heart create for me, O God" (v. 12), and the prophet Ezekiel reveals this telling plan of God: "I will give them a new heart" (Ezek. 11:19).

This new heart will be given definitively in Purgatory. That is where we hope to be fully purified. Pope Benedict XVI's words on the necessity of Purgatory are helpful here:

> I would go so far as to say that if there was no purgatory, then we would have to invent it, for who would dare say of himself that he was able to stand directly before God. And yet we don't want to be, to use an image from Scripture, "a pot that turned out wrong," that has to be thrown away; we want to be able to be put right. Purgatory basically means that God can put the pieces back together again. That He can cleanse us in such a way that we are able to be with Him and can stand there in the fullness of life. Purgatory strips off from one person what is unbearable and from another the inability to bear certain things, so that in each of them a pure heart is revealed, and we can see that we all belong together in one enormous symphony of being.[116]

[116] Benedict XVI, *God and the World: A Conversation with Peter Seewald* (San Francisco: Ignatius Press, 2002), 130–131.

Pope Benedict makes it clear that it is the activity of God that "can put the pieces back together again" and reveal in us "a pure heart." It is only God who can accomplish within us the beautiful work of a heart that is pure enough to see Him, to see Him as God is best seen, not with our eyes, but with our heart.

We cannot earn this gift.

We cannot create this gift.

It is God's gift to give.

Since it is a gift, however, it does need to be *received.*

It is necessary for us to cooperate with God in His desire for us to receive this gift. We are free to consent now to the path of purification necessary to see God "as he really is" (1 John 3:2). In Purgatory, the purification will take place without our further consent. Now we have the freedom to consent to each and every purifying act of God, making it all the more efficacious. The dark night is indeed God's gift. Purity of heart is not a gift reserved for the blessed in Heaven. The path is being opened for us to see God *now.*

The Dark Night vs. Darkness of Sin

During another presentation on the same topic, one sister quipped, "Doesn't everyone go through the dark night?" So, the next point worth our observation is to explain the difference between what we might call the "darkness of sin," that everyone does experience, and the dark night as described by St. John of the Cross.

The dark night is the activity of God drawing a beginner deeper into prayer through the path of purification. A beginner, by St. John's standards, is one who practices meditation.

The darkness of sin is something everyone will experience, even those who are not regularly praying. Through personal sin or the sin of those around us, we enter into true darkness and experience deep suffering. In those dark experiences many souls do go deeper in their relationship with God. The point at hand being, this dark experience of sin is not the activity of God in the dark night.

The Dark Night vs. Desolation

There is a term so commonly used in spiritual theology that is worth our examination. *The Spiritual Exercises* of St. Ignatius of Loyola refer to the experience of *desolation*. Both desolation and the purifying activity of God in the dark night are experienced as an absence of God. It is by their fruits that the difference between these two is known.

The dark night may *feel* like desolation. It might seem like God has abandoned us.

- ✠ When this is desolation, it will lead us away from God and weaken our trust in Him.
- ✠ An experience of desolation is to be rejected.
- ✠ When this is the dark night, our trust in God will be deepened.
- ✠ This purifying activity of God in the dark night is something we are free to give our consent to.

These telling words of Job in the midst of his purifying dark night might help us to appreciate the difference: "Although he slay me, I will trust him" (Job 13:15). A good spiritual director will also be of invaluable assistance in making this distinction between the experience of desolation and the activity of God in the dark night. Left alone, we often become confused as to which one is being experienced. One might think they are in the dark night when they are really going through desolation, while those experiencing the dark night might never guess what is actually occurring.

Does this Really Apply to All of Us, or Just for the Cloistered Carmelite?

There can be a misconception that these writings of St. John of the Cross are just for Carmelites, or for "monks who live in cells" as one sister put it. Again, it is the Church who recommends these writings for everyone. *The Dark Night* will prove beneficial to anyone making the effort to spend time with God in the midst of a busy schedule. When we finally succeed in setting aside a certain part of each day to pray, the experience will begin as one of great delight. When that delight begins to fade and every avenue of consolation seems to be closing, we might be tempted to question this effort to carve out time for daily prayer. That is why it is important for us to appreciate how this absence of consolation in prayer may just be the activity of God in the dark night. How necessary it is in the spiritual life to have some basic understanding of how God will eventually lead our soul into an experience of Him that is way beyond consolations.

How the Dark Night Unfolded for St. John of the Cross

The path by which St. John of the Cross was drawn into the very depths of God's love did not unfold in the manner he envisioned as a young friar. Shortly after his ordination as a Carmelite priest, Madre Teresa of Jesus, Teresa of Ávila's religious name in Spanish, had arranged a meeting with him to seek his assistance in extending her plan of reform for the Spanish Carmelites to the friars. Fray John (*fray* being Spanish for "friar") had set his sights on a more tranquil environment in which his soul might flourish. He related to her that he was seriously considering a transfer to the Carthusian Order. As mentioned earlier, the Carthusians have never been in need of a reform. She prevailed upon him to continue to seek a life of solitude and prayer without leaving "Our Lady's Order."

It was the fall of 1568; she was fifty-two and he was twenty-five. His young zeal was stoked by her steadfast, holy vision, but on the condition that he would not have to wait too long. Madre Teresa was true to her promise. Within a year, Fray John and four other companions converted a little farmhouse into a monastery with the intention of reforming to an observance the Carmelite Primitive Rule. They were soon referred to as *Discalced Carmelites,* for they went around barefoot. The term *discalced* (no shoes) seems fitting, for few of us would want to walk in the shoes of Fray John.

It was not in the company of these newly formed friars that he entered the "night that has united the Lover with His beloved, transforming the beloved in her Lover."[117] It was likewise not in his subsequent position as vicar and confessor to Madre Teresa's Convent of the Incarnation that he was able to experience his "house being now all stilled."[118] It was truly "in darkness and concealment"[119] that "all things ceased" as his own misguided brothers had him arrested, imprisoned, and left "forgotten among the lilies"[120] that Fray John was brought to the "place where no one else appeared," "where He waited for me — Him I knew so well."[121]

His own "ascent to Mount Carmel" was not sketched out in the joy of a newly formed community of brothers, or in the consolation of the good reformed sisters of Incarnation Convent. It was in the *nada, nada, nada* (in Spanish, "nothing, nothing, nothing") of a six-by-ten-foot closet into which his own brother Carmelites imprisoned him and apparently left him for dead.

[117] St. John of the Cross, *The Collected Works of St. John of the Cross, The Dark Night,* Prologue, Stanzas of the Soul, stanza 5.

[118] Ibid., stanza 1.

[119] Ibid., stanza 2

[120] Ibid., stanza 8.

[121] Ibid., stanza 4.

St. John of the Cross writes as a witness to the living martyrdom that painfully separates the soul from the familiar path of seeking God through the gifts of His consolation and the complete surrender to His mysterious hand at work in our soul. Fray John is no mere academic when he observes how in the beginning of our spiritual journey, "God nurtures and caresses the soul, after it has been resolutely converted to His service."[122] It is the poet in him that likens God's treatment of the soul to that of a "loving mother who warms her child with the heat of her bosom, nurses it with good milk and tender food, and carries and caresses it in her arms."[123] His skills as a spiritual director enable him to recognize that this "experience [of] intense satisfaction in the performance of spiritual exercises"[124] has yet to be "conditioned by the arduous struggle of practicing virtue."[125]

For it is precisely when "they are going about their spiritual exercises with delight and satisfaction, when in their opinion the sun of divine favor is shining most brightly upon them, that God darkens all this light and closes the door and spring of sweet spiritual water they were tasting as often and as long as they desired."[126] God sees that the soul is now ready for Him to transfer "His goods and strength from sense to spirit."[127]

The process by which God transfers "His goods and strength from sense to spirit" is described for us in book one of *The Dark Night*. It might be helpful to recall the diagram at the beginning of this book. What St. John is about to explain to us is the process by

[122] St. John of the Cross, *The Dark Night*, 1.1.2.

[123] Ibid.

[124] Ibid.

[125] Ibid., 1.1.3

[126] Ibid., 1.8.3.

[127] Ibid., 1.9.4.

which our experience of God is transferred from the *house of our senses* into the *interior castle of our soul.* When these goods and strength of God are experienced in the spirit, we call this *contemplative prayer*. Contemplative prayer is the gift of God we receive at the level of our spirit. To receive this gift, we need to be led beyond what we have come to know of God at the level of our senses.

"The Dark Night" was a poem likely composed by John while being imprisoned by his own brothers. It reflects the spiritual depths he was led to in this utterly purifying environment. Within Spanish poetry, his is appreciated as among the best of both religious and secular poems. What we are about to go through is the commentary John wrote on "The Dark Night" to better explain it. The poem in its entirety is found in appendix A. I recommend that you read this poem before we continue with the commentary.

Let us now allow this good Doctor to help prescribe for us the cure that will serve to purify our heart so that we might be led to enter into His rest.

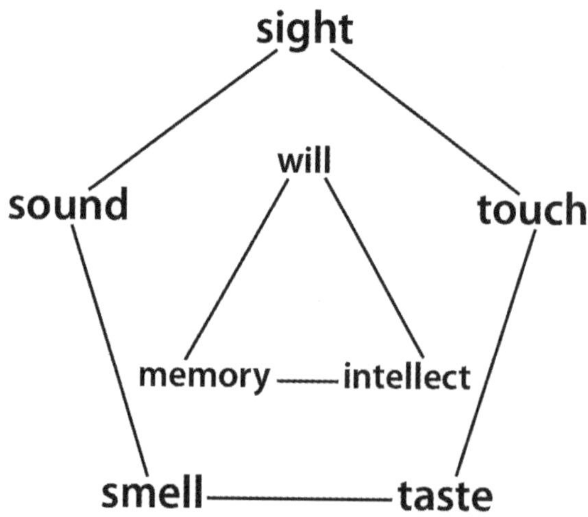

Chapter 8

The Dark Night: Book One

Book One of *The Dark Night* is addressed to "beginners" in the spiritual life. A beginner, by St. John's standard, is one who practices meditation regularly. By today's standards, they would practically be a guru. In fact, that is often the opinion they have of themselves. As St. Teresa observed in the third dwelling, some fall into the illusion that they are "lords of this world" after having denied themselves some of its pleasures and put into practice a daily regimen of prayer.

This first book of *The Dark Night* is addressed to beginners in the hope that they might understand themselves better. St. John gives three primary reasons for composing this commentary on *The Dark Night*:

✠ To help beginners "understand the feebleness of their state."

It is important to see ourselves as we are more truly seen by God. This revelation of our weaknesses is not meant to get us "stuck in the mud of our fears," as St. Teresa put it in her first dwelling. It is rather for the second reason John gives:

✠ To encourage them for the possibilities that still lie ahead.

There are miles to go in the spiritual journey. This is good news. Our experience of God can still grow. This leads us to the third reason:

✠ To give them "the desire that God place them in this night."

It is in this dark night that "the soul is strengthened in virtue and fortified for the inestimable delights of the love of God."

These three points are important to carry with us as St. John begins to walk us through the purifications that take place in our soul. This will help us through the times when we might feel discouraged. There will be moments when we can start to wonder why anyone in their right mind would want to be led into the dark night.

Part of the problem lies in our approach to prayer. Prayer is typically regarded as something *we* do. St. Teresa pointed out that we rarely consider what God does in prayer. When our experience of prayer authentically matures, the activity of God in our soul will become increasingly evident. Far from discouraging us, John is trying to arouse us to the grand possibilities that lie within as God begins the process of making us glorious in His sight (Isa. 49:5).

The soul of a beginner is "nurtured and caressed by God after it has been resolutely converted to His service." As mentioned previously, John likens God's care for the soul as "a loving mother who warms her child with the heat of her bosom, nurses it with good milk and tender food, and carries and caresses it in her arms," adding, "as the child grows older, the mother withholds her caresses and hides her tender love; she rubs bitter aloes on her sweet breast and sets the child down from her arms, letting it walk on its own feet so that it may put aside the habits of childhood and grow accustomed to greater and more important things."

A good mother knows when the time has come for her child to move past the stages of infancy. To keep nursing them until they are five years old would be doing them no favors. That doesn't stop the mother from giving her child the care they need as an infant.

In similar fashion, our Heavenly Father knows what is best for our soul. In the initial stages of the spiritual life, the soul "experiences intense satisfaction in performing spiritual exercises, because God is handing the breast of His tender love to the soul, just as if it were a delicate child. The soul finds its joy in spending lengthy periods at prayer, perhaps even entire nights; its penances are pleasures; its fasts, happiness; and the sacraments and spiritual conversations are its consolations."

Now is the time for such lavish nourishment. Our Heavenly Father is fully aware that their "motivation in their spiritual works and exercises is the consolation and satisfaction they experience in them." He realizes that "they have not yet been conditioned by the arduous struggle of practicing virtue and possess many faults and imperfections in the course of their spiritual activities." God knows they are still infants, and so He is happy to treat them as infants.

A principle that is important to bear in mind is that *God always does what is best for our soul.* When it is best for our soul to be treated as an infant, He treats us as an infant. When it is time for us to grow, He isn't afraid to allow the growing pains to set in.

The growing pains will likely set in as St. John begins to outline some of the imperfections of beginners. He uses the seven capital sins as his basis for identifying these spiritual imperfections. They are *spiritual* imperfections because they proceed from spiritual things. Spiritual gluttony is our over-indulging in the pleasures of things that are spiritual. When our imperfections stem from spiritual things, they are easily missed and even justified. It is important for us to become aware that these are imperfections. Then, when God begins to shine His light on the spiritual imperfections that are in us, we will be more ready to consent to the process by which our hearts are purified of them.

The Imperfections of Spiritual Pride

Chapter Two of **The Dark Night**, *Book One*

Despite the fact that spiritual works should cause humility, "a certain kind of secret pride" wells up within, making us complacent with our accomplishments and ourselves. We are easily deceived into thinking that we have already arrived at the top of the mountain in the spiritual life. We can succumb to vanity in liking "to speak of spiritual things in the presence of others, and sometimes even to instruct rather than to be instructed." We are tempted to find great pleasure in revealing to others what we know about the spiritual life, in the hope that it might enable them to see how "holy" we are. Our hearts fall into "condemning others who do not seem to have the kind of devotion we would like them to have, and we sometimes even openly express such criticism." This is all very much like the Pharisee who despised the publican while boasting and praising God for the good deeds he himself accomplished (Luke 18:11–12).

The devil is very happy to help beginners grow in pride and presumption. The evil one knows that spiritual works performed with pride "are not only worthless for us, but even become vices." Our vanity can become so strong that we desire "no one but ourselves to appear holy; and so by word and deed, condemn and detract others whenever the occasion arises." We can fail to consider the beam in our own eye (Matt. 7:3) or strain at the other's gnat and swallow our own camel (Matt. 23:24). It can become difficult for us to hear others being complimented. Our own desire for recognition can lead us to condemn them in our hearts. We may even give into sharing a few tidbits about this person that aren't so inspiring. This is all spiritual pride.

In our desire for others to recognize our spirit and devotion, we can even make little ceremonies out of our spiritual exercises, with the devil's assistance, and be pleased when others take notice of them. We easily forget how Jesus taught us to "take care not to perform righteous deeds in order that people may see them; otherwise, you will have no recompense from your heavenly Father" (Matt. 6:1). It is what Our Father sees in secret (Matt. 6:4) that He repays. When we allow spiritual pride to reveal the secret of our devotion, we deprive ourselves of what only our Heavenly Father can give us. What an empty reward it is to win the praise of others (see Matt. 6:2).

There is also a dangerous desire to "want to be the favorites of our confessors." We can "approach the confessional more to excuse ourselves than to accuse ourselves." Our sins might be confessed in a favorable light, to appear better than we actually are. At times, we minimize our faults or emphasize the faults of others. Sometimes we may even be too embarrassed to honestly confess our sins. The more evil matters might be put on hold to be confessed to a different confessor, or even go so far as to omit them from being confessed. The *Catechism* will remind us here that "if the sick person is too ashamed to show his wound to the doctor, the medicine cannot heal what it does not know."[128]

It is spiritual pride that makes us easily discouraged by the truth of our sins. It is not uncommon "to become impatient and angry with

[128] CCC 1456. Council of Trent (1551): DS 1680 (ND 1626); cf. St. Jerome, *In Eccl.* 10, 11: PL 23:1096.

ourself," not wanting to believe these sins are still inside of us. We "are often extremely anxious that God remove our faults and imperfections." If God did as we asked, we would be filled with even more pride and presumption.

When confronted by spiritual directors or good spiritual friends on our imperfections, we might feel they don't understand. What we are looking for from them is their praise and esteem. When they offer critical advice, our impure hearts don't regard them as being holy enough to really appreciate what is happening in our soul. As St. John puts it, "They flee, as they would from death, those who attempt to place them on the safe road."

All of this goes to prove that our motivation in the spiritual life is more about us than it is about God. We are more interested in our own spiritual growth, in apparent holiness, than we are about true union with God. The number of these imperfections in beginners varies, but "there are scarcely any beginners who do not fall victim to some of these imperfections at the time of their initial fervor."

A soul who is advancing in perfection will respond with humility during this period. Recall how St. Teresa observed in the third dwelling that "if humility is lacking, we will remain our whole life!" But when "humility (is) present, this stage is a most excellent one."

St. John recognizes how the soul growing in humility will "place little importance on their own deeds and take little self-satisfaction in them." "The more they do, the less satisfaction they derive from it." Whatever they do is done for God, and this seems like nothing at the moment. They never seem to notice what others think of them; they consider themselves to be insignificant and want others to think so, too. Even when others do praise them, they do not believe them. Such praise sounds strange to them, for they are aware of their imperfections. "They think everyone else is far better than themselves, and usually possess a holy envy of them and would like to emulate their service of God." "These souls humbly and tranquilly long to be taught by anyone who might help them. This desire is the exact opposite of that other desire we mentioned above, of those who want to be themselves the teachers in everything." The humble soul is "ready to take a road different from the one they are following, if told to do so." In spiritual direction "they are more eager to speak of faults and sins, and reveal these to others, than their virtues."

These are the characteristics of a soul being purified. They are aware of their own imperfections and don't have time to waste trying to impress anyone or judge them. They would likely never guess that they are in the dark night. That would seem a far too elevated spiritual place for them. It often proves that those who think they are in the dark night are often not, though those humble souls who everyone will readily recognize as being close to God, never seem to see in themselves how the purifying hand of God is at work in their souls.

The Imperfections of Spiritual Avarice (Greed)

Chapter Three of The Dark Night*, Book One*

Just as natural greed does not allow one to be content with having enough, so too, in spiritual greed one is never "content with the spirit God gives them." Spiritual avarice will make us impatient with "the lack of consolation we seem to receive from spiritual things." It can leave us constantly looking for a feeling. In our greed for consolations, we will devour books, breeze through devotions, run to every possible spiritual speaker, and so forth.

Spiritual avarice can also be outwardly manifested in the sheer number of religious articles we seem to need. Although we can only pray with one rosary at a time, we simply can't part with the other twelve around our home. Each one has a special feeling attached to it: this one is from Assisi, that one from Rome, another from Fatima, and this dear old one of my great-great-grandma. Our homes can become more ornate than shrines. Sometimes we ourselves become weighted down with all kinds of religious hardware hanging from our neck. The chains from our crucifix, miraculous medal, and St. Christopher medal become an entangled mess as they all clank around our neck, looking for a safe place to land.

From the outside, it might look like a good religious show. The problem is within. "Possessiveness of heart" is "contrary to poverty of spirit." Spiritual poverty is needed to keep us focused on the true purpose of prayer.

The dark night will eventually purify our heart of spiritual avarice by leaving in dryness all the pleasures we once found in our attachments to these instruments of devotion.

The Imperfections of Spiritual Lust

Chapter Four of **The Dark Night**, *Book One*

The term *spiritual lust* can be confusing. How could we possibly lust in a spiritual way? We can't. In this chapter, St. John is addressing the experience of human lust that can happen "during spiritual exercises, and even sometimes when the spirit is in deep prayer or when receiving the sacrament of penance or of the Eucharist." This experience of lust is not caused by a lack of virtue. It happens to a soul that is striving to please God.

St. John's clear dealing with this topic is most beneficial, as spiritual lust is rather glossed over due to the shame associated with it.

When the experience of lust is not the result of our own sinful inclinations, it can arise from any one of the following three causes:

✠ "From the pleasure one finds in spiritual exercises"

In our spiritual exercises, God is touching both the *sensory* part and the *spiritual* part of our soul. What is happening at the higher, spiritual level is beyond "what eye can see and ear can hear" (see 1 Cor. 2:9). The lower, sensual part of the soul holds on to what the senses know about intimacy.

It might be helpful to recall how in the act of marital love, the two become one at both the physical and spiritual levels. The physical typically gets most of the attention. It requires a pure heart to appreciate the spiritual union, which the act of marital love is really all about.

A similar movement is now happening in our soul. God is preparing our soul to become one with Him. At the beginning stages of this union, spiritual lust can sometimes happen as the lower, sensual part of the soul is aroused by what it experiences in the union of the two becoming one. John refers to this lust as a type of rebellion of the lower part of the soul — a rebellion because the process of union with God is unfolding in the soul, and the senses hold on to what they know about union. This can be distracting and disturbing. It all takes time to purify. The soul will eventually get this straightened out in the dark night, as it learns to receive the Spirit of God in the midst of utter dryness.

✠ "The second origin of these rebellions is the devil"

The devil tries to distract us from our efforts to pray by tempting us with lustful thoughts and feelings in the sensory part of the soul. "The devil excites these feelings while souls are at prayer, instead of when they are engaged in works, so that they might abandon prayer." His evil desire is to jar us out of our efforts to be quiet and still. It works.

It is important to realize how these temptations differ from the lust brought on by our own sin. If, prior to entering into prayer, we were dabbling with lustful thoughts or immodest images, then we need to be more self-disciplined.

On the other hand, when these lustful thoughts enter our time of prayer without our assistance, "if a person pays any attention to them, the devil does him great harm." "Some souls, through fear, grow slack in their prayer — which is what the devil wants."

Do not be surprised by what the evil one will do to drive us away from prayer or receiving a sacrament. These lustful temptations need to be given straight to the Lord as soon as they come. God knows a thought before it is ever on our mind. Give it to Him and remain in His love.

✠ Fear of these thoughts

The very fear of having such thoughts during times of prayer can itself be the impetus through which they come. A person who is deathly afraid of having a car accident is actually more prone to causing one. In the same manner, the soul who stands in anxious fear of having lustful thoughts can be making them all the more likely to occur.

It is important to accept our very human condition and the truth that we are likely to struggle with lustful thoughts throughout our entire life. There is the story of an eighty-year old priest who once sent out an invitation for a party to celebrate the end of his struggle with lust. Two weeks later, a cancellation notice was issued.

It has been commented that our struggle with lust will end thirty minutes after we are dead. So don't be too surprised by these temptations. Just be sure to give them straight to God as soon as they come.

Spiritual Friendships

St. John then addresses some helpful words on the lust that can happen in good spiritual friendships. The attraction begins on a spiritual level. We remain human, however, and the senses have a way of pulling our attraction down to their level.

St. John observes that when our contact with a certain person leaves us thinking more about them than about God, then it is a matter of spiritual lust. "This lustful origin will be recognized if, upon recalling that affection, there is not an increase in the remembrance and love of God, but remorse of conscience." On the other hand, "the affection is purely spiritual if the love of God grows when it grows, or if the love of God is remembered as often as the affection is remembered, or if the affection gives the soul a desire for God."

In a spiritual friendship, contact with this person will fire our soul with a greater desire for God. Even good spiritual friendships are not immune to the natural level of affection. In the spiritually mature there will be a process of purification. If, on the other hand, even one of the individuals remains unwilling to deny the more sensual desires, great care must be taken to avoid any further contact that would only result in serious harm to one or both of their souls.

It is a very common experience for lust to creep into good spiritual relationships. Everyone falls in *luv* again. Notice the word *luv* and not *love.*

> *Luv* is those warm, fuzzy feelings we all so enjoy.
>
> *Love* is the resolve of our will to do what is best for the soul of the beloved.

Even after we make our life commitment of *love*, there will still be encounters of *luv*. It is then that the commitment of *love* must come to the rescue with a resolve to sacrifice these desires of *luv*. In religious life, when *luv* comes knocking, it is our *love* for God that must answer. In married life, every other *luv* will need to be sacrificed for the sake of the one you have promised to *love* and honor all the days of your life.

Here are some good principles with which to examine our conscience in spiritual friendships:

> Am I looking for something from this friend that I should only be looking for from God (or my spouse)?
>
> Am I trying to offer this friend what they should only be receiving from God (or their spouse)?

The final word in this chapter is that the dark night puts all of these loves back in order by depriving our senses of all such consolations.

The Imperfections of Spiritual Anger

Chapter Five of *The Dark Night, Book One*

Anger, of itself, is not a vice. St. Thomas Aquinas taught that the object of anger is good, for it seeks justice.[129] We normally get angry over what we regard as an injustice. How we go about addressing that injustice will reveal a heart that is either virtuous or vicious.

[129] St. Thomas Aquinas, *Summa Theologica*, I-II, q. 46, art. 2.

A wise spiritual man once reflected that there is not much you can do about your emotions. How you feel is how you feel. Anger is an emotion. What you do with these emotions remains in your control. It is our attitude for which we must render an account.

St. John recognizes that "because of the strong desire of many beginners for spiritual gratification, they usually have many imperfections of anger."

He describes three ways in which we will all likely experience spiritual anger:

- ✠ The first type of spiritual anger arises "when the delight in spiritual exercises passes." Our initial experience of dryness in prayer is typically met with anger. It seems an injustice. As a result, "they become peevish in the works they do and easily angered by the least thing, and occasionally they are so unbearable that nobody can put up with them." St. John explains that this frequently happens after a pleasant experience in prayer. When the experience comes to an end, we can become "as a child withdrawn from the sweet breast." "These souls are not at fault if they do not allow this dejection to influence them, for it is an imperfection which must be purged through the dryness and distress of the dark night."

- ✠ The second type of spiritual anger is "a certain indiscreet zeal at the sins of others." There are, of course, sins for which we should become angry. This anger, however, might lead us to forming judgments about another person's soul. Sometimes we "set ourselves up as lords of virtue" and angrily reprove others. St. John recognizes that this is all "contrary to spiritual meekness." There is a proper manner for giving good, virtuous, fraternal correction. Anger will likely awaken us to the need for such corrections. How we carry out those corrections will reveal whether our heart is being guided by virtue or by vice. St. John Bosco used to advise his fellow co-workers in their dealing with troubled youth to first discipline themselves before they discipline the children. Otherwise they may simply "send forth a flood of words that will only offend the listener and have no effect on those who are guilty." "There must be no hostility in our minds, no contempt in our eyes, no insult on our lips."[130]

✠ The third type of spiritual anger is impatience with our own imperfections. We "want to become a saint in a day!" There is a tendency to think that we are holier than we actually are. When we keep committing the same sins over and over, we can get angry with ourselves. Sometimes we even get angry with God for not taking away those temptations. It is important to learn humble patience. St. John observes that many beginners make "numerous plans and great resolutions, but since they are not humble and have no distrust of themselves, the more resolves they make the more they break, and the greater becomes their anger." Holiness is an exercise in humility. God alone is the holy one, and we must "wait until God gives us what we need when He so desires." This impatience is all "contrary to spiritual meekness" and "can only be remedied by the purgation of the dark night."

St. John then makes this final telling observation: "Some, however, are so patient about their desire for advancement that God would prefer to see them a little less so."

[130] From a letter by St. John Bosco as found in volume 3 of the Liturgy of the Hours, p. 1338.

The Imperfections of Spiritual Gluttony

Chapter Six of The Dark Night, *Book One*

"A great deal can be said on spiritual gluttony." "There is hardly a beginner who does not fall into some of the many imperfections of this vice. These imperfections arise because of the delight found in spiritual exercises."

Spiritual gluttony acts very much like natural gluttony; they both attempt to lure us away from the true purpose of what we are doing and into doing it merely for pleasure. Natural gluttony tempts us to eat more than is necessary for our nourishment and neglect to eat the foods our body needs. Spiritual gluttony will tempt us to perform spiritual exercises for the sole purpose of receiving consolations.

St. John's examination of spiritual gluttony bears some similarities to spiritual avarice. The spiritual glutton, like the spiritually greedy, just can't get enough spiritual consolations. "The sweetness these persons experience makes them go to extremes and pass beyond the mean in which virtue resides and is acquired."

The beginner will devour spiritual books and constantly change the topics of their meditation, always looking for some gratification. The glutton will "kill themselves with penances, weaken themselves with fasts" because they find these activities so enjoyable. They neglect to seek counsel that might keep them from going beyond what is good for their soul and end up "overtaxing their weaknesses."

The difference in these two vices lies in what drives one to the extreme:

- ✠ In *avarice*, it is *discontentment*. They are never satisfied with what is being given.
- ✠ In *gluttony*, it is an *inability to be content*. They cannot get enough.

There is also difference in the virtue that will help drive these vices away.

- ✠ Spiritual avarice is opposed to *spiritual poverty.*
- ✠ Spiritual gluttony wants to remain a stranger to *spiritual sobriety.*

Spiritual sobriety is an often-forgotten virtue. We all prefer the more intoxicating experiences of the spiritual life. They are given to strengthen us for the sobering journey that lies ahead. Jesus knew that Peter, James, and John needed the intoxicating experience of the Transfiguration to strengthen them for the sobering way of the Cross that lay ahead of them (Matt. 17:1–13).

The addictive nature of spiritual gluttony is revealed in how a beginner can "try to hide their penances from those they owe obedience to in such matters. Some even dare perform these penances contrary to obedience." They lose sight of how the only acceptable sacrifice to God is a "humble, contrite heart" (Ps. 51:19).

St. John goes so far as to call penance without obedience the "penance of the beasts." The entire purpose of penance, as the Carthusians taught us back in part one, was to create "an emptiness, a listening ear, a heart that is attentive."[131] Like St. Paul, we discipline and train ourselves (1 Cor. 9:27) so that, like Jesus, we might do not our own will but the will of the one who sends us (John 6:38). Obedience is the offering more pleasing and acceptable to God than any other sacrifice made in an effort to atone for sin (1 Sam. 15:22).

To keep us from being obedient, the devil will try to "increase the delights and appetites of these beginners." Then, when "they are unable to avoid obedience, they either add to, change, or modify what was commanded them." Any obedience becomes distasteful to

[131] A Carthusian, *The Way of Silent Love,* 91.

them. "Some will reach a point that the mere obligation of obedience to perform their spiritual exercises makes them lose all desire and devotion." For a consecrated religious, community prayers might seem monotonous. Even the Mass that they are obliged to attend loses its appeal in sight of the opportunity to go somewhere else. "Their only yearning and satisfaction is to do what they feel inclined to do, whereas it would be better in all likelihood for them not to do this at all."

The beginners St. John is speaking of "are under the impression that they don't serve God when they are not allowed to do what they want." "Since they take gratification and their own will as their support and their god, they become sad, weak, and discouraged when their director takes these from them and desires that they do God's will." They are deceived into thinking that "gratifying and satisfying themselves is serving and satisfying God."

It is easy for a beginner to fall under the impression that something is wrong when nothing is *felt* in prayer. They can "think the whole matter of prayer consists in looking for sensory satisfaction." When prayer becomes dry, it is considered a waste of time. Even in their reception of Holy Communion, they "spend all their time trying to get some feeling and satisfaction rather than humbly praising and reverencing God."

Our Lord lovingly denies satisfaction to these beginners in order to purge them of the selfishness with which they are seeking Him. He will even withdraw the sensory delights of Holy Communion to try and refocus them on the invisible, lasting graces. "Spiritual sobriety and temperance beget very different qualities." These are the qualities that will bear fruit that will last (John 15:16).

When we come to recognize the spiritual glutton within us, the key is to practice self-denial and submissiveness in all things "until God in fact puts us into the dark night and purifies us."

The Imperfections of Spiritual Envy and Sloth

Chapter Seven of The Dark Night*, Book One*

The true face of evil is shown in the sad countenances of those who fall prey to these final two vices: envy and sloth.

Sloth is the sadness that falls upon us as we behold how rough and narrow is the path that leads to purity of heart.

Envy is the sad truth that others are well ahead of us on that road to perfection.

St. John deals with envy first.

Envy is the sadness we experience in the face of another's spiritual goodness. It is no small grief to know that others are ahead of us on the road to perfection. The beginner "will not want to hear others praised. To learn of the virtues of others makes them sad; they cannot bear to hear others praised without contradicting and undoing these compliments as much as possible. Their annoyance grows because they themselves do not receive these plaudits and because they long for preference in everything." This is all quite contrary to the love Jesus taught us to have for even our enemies (Matt. 5:44).

Sloth is an often misunderstood (and mispronounced) vice. *Slōth* is normally considered as almost a synonym for laziness and idleness — an idle mind is the devil's workshop. We tend to regard a slothful person as a lazy person.

Classical theology gives sloth another word (and a variety of pronunciations). *Acedia* (ā-sē-dē, ä; or the Greek ακέδιά) is defined as a kind of sadness. St. John of the Cross recognizes the sadness of *acedia* as an aversion to having to do the will of God when it doesn't bring immediate gratification. We are tempted to "run from anything rough and are scandalized by the cross." The opposite of *acedia* is not "working hard," for we can work hard to avoid the cross. The opposite of acedia is an often-forgotten virtue called *magnanimity*.

A *magnanimous* heart is one that is open to the truly great human potential: to have a pure heart that can see God. The sorrow of *acedia* lacks courage for the great things that are proper to a Christian. One who is trapped in *acedia* has neither the courage nor the will to be as great as he really is.

St. John recognizes *acedia* in beginners as they "become weary in the more spiritual exercises and flee from them, since these exercises are contrary to sensory satisfaction. Since they are so used to finding delight in spiritual practices, they become bored when they do not find it. If they do not receive in prayer the satisfaction they crave — they do not want to return to it."

When dryness sets into the time of prayer, a beginner can work very hard at finding "good" reasons to avoid having to sit through another boring hour of prayer. "They subordinate the way of perfection to the pleasure and delight of their own will. As a result they strive to satisfy their own will rather than God's." It is not uncommon to set our own standard for discipleship, and it is not self-denial and sacrifice. To follow Jesus, we must deny our self and pick up our cross.

It might be worth noting that in the Greek, *ακέδιά* comes from the combination of α — not, and κεδος — care, that is, *I don't care*! God has opened up to us the possibility of being one with Him, but the sight of how "rough and narrow" (Matt. 7:14) is the road that leads to purity of heart leaves us with no real desire to actually walk it.

An experience of *acedia* is well described by Abba Cassian:

> Once when I was talking to some brothers on a helpful topic, they were overcome by sleep so deep, that they could not even move their eyelids any longer. Then, wishing to show them the power of the devil, I introduced a trivial subject of conversation.

> Immediately, they woke up, full of joy. Then I said to them with many sighs, "until now, we were discussing heavenly things and your eyes were heavy with sleep, when I embarked on a useless discourse, you all woke up with alacrity (liveliness). Therefore, brothers, I implore you to recognize the power of the evil demon; pay attention to yourselves, and guard yourselves from the desire to sleep when you are doing or listening to something spiritual."[132]

Acedia is perhaps best described by Evagrius Ponticus as the "devil of the noonday sun." Although the following quote is quite lengthy, I am confident that you will not be sad to read it in its entirety:

> The demon of *acedia*—also called the noonday demon—is the one that causes the most serious trouble of all. He presses his attack upon the monk about the fourth hour (10 a.m.) and besieges the soul until the eighth hour (2 p.m.). First of all, he makes it seem that the sun barely moves, if at all, and that the day is fifty hours long. Then he constrains the monk to look constantly out the windows, to walk outside the cell, to gaze carefully at the sun to see how far it stands from the ninth hour (3 p.m.), to look now this way and now that to see if perhaps [one of the brethren appears from his cell]. Then too he instills in the heart of the monk a hatred for the place, a hatred for his very life itself, a hatred for manual labor. He leads him to reflect that charity has

132 Abba Cassian, *The Sayings of the Desert Fathers* (Kalamazoo, MI: Cistercian, 1984), 114, par. 6.

> departed from among the brethren, that there is no one to give encouragement. Should there be someone at this period who happens to offend him in some way or other; this too the demon uses to contribute further to his hatred. This demon drives him along to desire other sites where he can more easily procure life's necessities, more readily find work and make a real success of himself. He goes on to suggest that, after all, it is not the place that is the basis of pleasing the Lord. God is to be adored everywhere. He joins to these reflections the memory of his dear ones and of his former way of life. He depicts life stretching out for a long period of time, and brings before the mind's eye the toil of the ascetic struggle and, as the saying has it, leaves no leaf unturned to induce the monk to forsake his cell and drop out of the fight. No other demon follows close upon the heels of this one (when he is defeated) but only a state of deep peace and inexpressible joy arise out of this struggle.[133]

To experience that deep peace and inexpressible joy, the need for God to wean these beginners from the breasts of gratifications and delights and make them grow in virtue is becoming all too evident.

The stage is now at last set for St. John of the Cross, the Mystical Doctor of the Church, to open up for us the deep meaning of his poem that has left such an enduring mark on Christian spirituality.

The succeeding chapters are a line-by-line commentary on the first verse of his poem, *The Dark Night*. The first line begins, "One dark night."

[133] Evagrius Ponticus, *The Praktikos,* no. 12.

The Beginning of the Exposition of *The Dark Night*

Chapter Eight of The Dark Night, *Book One*

An Explanation of Verse One of the First Stanza

"This night, which as we say is contemplation." It is very important to appreciate that St. John clearly identifies the dark night as the beginning of contemplation. The dark night is the activity of God in our soul working to break through our attachment to the mere activity of man in prayer. In the telling words of St. Teresa's fourth dwelling, the "supernatural experiences begin here."[134]

This night "causes two kinds of darkness, or purgation, in spiritual persons according to the two parts of the soul, the *sensory* and the *spiritual*."

- ✠ "One night, or purgation, is *sensory*, by which our senses are purged and accommodated to the *spirit*."
- ✠ "The other night, or purgation, will be *spiritual*, by which the spirit is purged and denuded as well as accommodated and prepared for union with God through love."
- ✠ "The *sensory night* is common and happens to many."
- ✠ "*The spiritual night* is the lot of very few, of those who have been tried and are proficient."

It is critical to bear in mind the very positive purpose for this process of purgation.

The first night serves to purify our attachment to the senses so that we might enjoy the ways of the spirit, where the gift of contemplation is received.

[134] St. Teresa of Ávila, *The Interior Castle*, 4.1.1.

The second night prepares us for union with God.

The beautiful purpose of these purgations must be kept firmly in mind as St. John goes on to remark, "The first night of purgation is bitter and terrible to the senses, but nothing compared to the second, for it is horrible and frightful to the spirit." I am sure that makes us all excited to be led into these purgations. Yet if our desire is for union with God, indeed, bring it on!

St. John's writings on the first night are brief in comparison to the second night of the spirit. He regards the first night as more commonly experienced and written about. The second night is dealt with at more length, "for hardly anything has been said of it, in sermons or in writing, and even the experience of it is rare." This remains true five hundred years later. In fact, today hardly anything even seems to be said of the first night.

The first night occurs "after beginners have exercised themselves for a time in the way of virtue and have persevered in meditation and prayer." Referring back to St. Teresa's *Interior Castle,* in the third dwelling God comforts the soul for having turned to Him. To help strengthen our resolve and gain some spiritual strength, God fills our experience of prayer with delight and satisfaction. God realizes that beginners are not too distant from love of self and gratifications. Before He is able to lead them to a higher degree of love, it is first necessary for them to "persevere in this practice of prayer and meditation."

As we begin to master our passions for some of the world's allurements, we can think we have reached the top of this spiritual mountain, regarding ourselves, as St. Teresa put it, as "lords of this world."

St. John observes that it is precisely at this moment "when in their opinion the sun of divine favor is shining most brightly upon them, that God darkens all this light and closes the door and spring of the sweet spiritual water they were tasting as often and as long as they desired." We had previously been too weak and tender for any door to be closed to us.

"When God sees that they have grown a little, He weans them from the sweet breast so that they might be strengthened, lays aside their swaddling bands, and puts them down from His arms that they may grow accustomed to walking by themselves. This change is a surprise to them because everything seems to be functioning in reverse."

The image of being weaned is insightful. A child normally struggles with the initial process of being weaned. They don't think it is such a good idea. A mother once related how she would nurse her child in the same chair every day. When the time came for weaning, this little one would walk over to the chair, look at her mom, and pat the chair, beckoning her to come. In the same way, we can find ourselves trying to beckon God to return to our favorite prayer place with the hope that He might pacify us once again with such sweet consolations. A good mother and our Heavenly Father know when it is time for their child to be weaned.

When that time comes, God leaves our soul in such darkness that we will not know what to do in prayer. We will no longer be able to meditate. "He leaves them in such dryness that they not only fail to receive satisfaction and pleasure from their spiritual exercises and works, as they formerly did, but also find these exercises distasteful and bitter."

"Not much time normally passes after the initial stages of their spiritual life before beginners start to enter this night of sense."

That is why it is so important for us to have some understanding of what is happening in our life of prayer. St. John will soon guide us as to what we should do when this purgation begins. First, he will help us to discern whether this dryness in prayer is truly the dark night. It could be the result of sin, some weakness, or just becoming lukewarm. The next chapter is most important in helping souls to make a proper discernment of whether what they are experiencing in prayer is the dark night. Many souls will think they are in the dark night when they are not, while other souls might think they have lost their way when the hand of God is actually upon them.

Signs for Discerning whether a Spiritual Person is Treading the Path of This Sensory Night and Purgation

Chapter Nine of The Dark Night*, Book One*

This chapter merits our full attention. St. John of the Cross will now clearly spell out for us how to discern whether it is truly the hand of God leading us into "this sensory night and purgation." "Because the origin of these aridities may not be the sensory night and purgation, but sin and imperfection, or weakness and lukewarmness, or some bad humor or bodily illness."

St. John gives three principal signs for discerning whether this dryness is the result of the purgation or of one of these other defects.

1) **No satisfaction or consolation is found in the things of God or from creatures.** God's intent is to dry up and completely purge our sensory appetite in both a spiritual and natural way. So "He does not allow the soul to find sweetness or delight in anything." The time we spend in prayer will be left in utter dryness. Even our spiritual works will bring no satisfaction. If this were the result of sin, the temptation would remain for us to return to the satisfaction we had found in the things of creation. When the hand of God is upon us, no consolation will be found even there. This

sign alone is not enough for us to determine whether it is the dark night. It could be that some type of depression has set in, "which frequently prevents one from being satisfied with anything." In the grips of depression, one is unable to find consolation in anything. This second sign is necessary to help us distinguish what is happening.

2) **"The memory ordinarily turns to God solicitously and with painful care."** The soul is aware that it has lost its taste for the things of God. It is painful to the one being purified to think that they are not serving God and are somehow turning back in the spiritual life. This would not be a concern for one who is lazy, lukewarm, or depressed. A lazy person would not make the effort to turn to God with "painful care." The lukewarm is not over-concerned about serving God. A soul fallen into depression typically just wants to stay in bed.

   The soul ready to be purified by the hand of God will not falter in their desire to serve Him. This doesn't mean they won't go through moments when they simply want to throw their hands up in frustration. It also doesn't mean that God can't use an experience of depression to further purify a soul that is ready, as He often does. What it means is that through whatever God might send, the prevailing, underlying disposition of a soul being purified is a deep resolution to please God.

This disposition is clearly reflected in the private writings of St. Teresa of Calcutta. The pain she expresses is so heartfelt that it is almost difficult to read. Let us listen to what it sounds like when "the memory turns to God solicitously and with painful care":

> I want God with all the powers of my soul — and yet there between us — there is terrible separation. I don't pray any longer — I utter words of community prayers — and try my utmost to get out of every word the sweetness it has to give — but my prayer of union is not there any longer — I no longer pray.
>
> Jesus, don't let my soul be deceived — nor let me deceive anyone. In the call You said I would have to suffer much — ten years — my Jesus, You have done to me according to Your will — and Jesus hear my prayer — if this pleases You — if my pain and suffering — my darkness and separation gives You a drop of consolation — my own Jesus, do with me as You wish — as long as You wish, without a single glance at my feelings and pain. I am Your own.[135]

St. John explains that "the reason for this dryness is that God transfers His goods and strengths from senses to spirit." Referring to the diagram at the beginning of this book, God is moving our experience of Him from the *house of our senses* to *the interior castle of our soul.*

"Since the sensory part of the soul is incapable of the goods of spirit, it remains deprived, dry, and empty." By leaving our senses in complete dryness, we slowly become accustomed to having our spirit nourished more purely by God. This subtle taste of the spirit

[135] St. Teresa of Calcutta, *Come Be My Light*, ed. Brian Kolodiejchuk (New York: Doubleday, 2007) 193–194.

can take some time to appreciate as "our palate is accustomed to these other sensory tastes."

St. John likens a soul being purified to the children of Israel, whom God "led into the desert solitude in order to begin nourishing them with heavenly food ... yet they nonetheless felt a craving for the tastes of the flesh meats they had eaten in Egypt." "In the midst of heavenly food, they wept and sighed for flesh meat" (see Num. 11:4–6).

We, too, can continue to weep and sigh even as God begins to nourish our soul with heavenly food. Although the food of contemplation is first experienced as being dark and dry to the senses, hidden from the very one receiving it, an inclination will arise deep within them to remain alone and in quiet. There is a longing desire in the soul to be alone with God, even though His presence is not *felt*. As St. Teresa of Calcutta revealed in her private writings, "I wish I could go somewhere alone — to be alone with God even though He may not want to be alone with me."[136]

The soul begins to recognize how prayer is strengthening them without giving delight. This new nourishment is beyond "what eye can see and ear can hear." As one sister on a retreat wisely put it, "I don't always know what happens in prayer, but I know what happens when I don't pray."

This is why St. John's exposition of *The Dark Night* is so imperative, for it can seem to a soul that they should keep trying to return to what they know about prayer. Our senses are craving the path by which they had previously received consolations, even though Our Lord places deep within us a desire to just be still. To those who can simply surrender to remaining quiet, "without care about any interior or exterior work, they will soon in that unconcern and idleness

[136] Ibid., 243.

delicately experience interior nourishment." This heavenly nourishment is "so delicate, that usually if a soul desires or tries to experience it, it cannot"; it comes unknowingly. It is all quite contrary to the beginning of the spiritual life. The effort to pray with your faculties will actually hinder the soul in this state.

It is now God who works in our soul. *It is what God does in prayer.*

He "binds the interior faculties and leaves no support in the intellect, nor satisfaction in the will, nor remembrance in the memory." We will even "be unable to dwell upon any particular thought, nor will we have the desire to do so."

This binding of the interior faculties reminds us of what St. Teresa wrote about the faculties being "suspended" in the *prayer of quiet*. God sees that we are now ready for Him to work in our soul, so He touches our soul in such a way that the best we can do is "be still and know that I am God" (Ps. 46:11). The new delights He is giving are far different from all the gratifications we received as a beginner. It is now a "tiny whispering breeze" (1 Kings 19:12), whose "fruit is quiet, delicate, solitary, satisfying and peaceful."

3) **Powerlessness.** The third sign that this is all the hand of God is that in spite of one's efforts to pray or meditate, "God will not communicate Himself through the senses as He did before by means of discursive analysis and synthesis of ideas." *Discursive analysis and synthesis of ideas* are what occur in our mind during meditation. We analyze the ways of God revealed through Sacred Scripture and the lives of the saints and come up with ideas about how it applies to our own spiritual journey with Christ. Now "God begins to communicate Himself through pure spirit by an act of simple contemplation, in which there is no discursive succession of thought."

> "At this time God does not communicate Himself through the senses as He did before."

The "lower part of the soul cannot attain to this contemplation." Now is the time for God to extend to us the gift of contemplation, which the sensory part of our soul is unable to experience. God, who is light, departs from there, leaving it in darkness.

This third sign will help us to discern how this dryness in prayer is "not the fruit of any bad humor." "If it were, a person would be able with little care to return to his former exercises and find support for his faculties when that humor passed away." When the hand of God is upon us purifying the appetite of our senses, "this return is not possible."

If a soul is not ready to be purified all at once, it is at times given the ability to return to meditation. St. John remarks that not everyone can be weaned all at once. God works in a way that is best for each soul. He is patient for them to gain the strength needed to leave behind the work of their senses.

There are some who remain too weak to truly walk the road of contemplation. The night of dryness is not as continuous for them. They can meditate at times and at other times they cannot. "God places them in this night solely to exercise and humble them." "God does not bring to contemplation all those who purposely exercise themselves in the way of the spirit, nor even half. Why? God knows best."

Contemplation always remains God's gift to give. He will only give it when it will not harm the soul. As we are wisely advised in the Song of Songs, God knows to "not stir up or awaken love before its time" (8:4).

Now that we know how to discern when it is the love of God being stirred up, how ought one respond to such an awakening?

The Conduct Required of a Soul in This Dark Night

Chapter Ten of The Dark Night, *Book One*

God is awakening our soul to His presence within, drawing us away from our practice of meditation in order to receive His gift of contemplation. In contemplation "the soul no longer has power to work or meditate with its faculties on the things of God." As had been mentioned, this will be the cause of considerable suffering in spiritual persons. They will fear having gone astray. The persisting dryness in prayer can make them believe that "there will be no more spiritual blessings and that God has abandoned them."

As we pray in the Psalms, "Your favor had set me on a mountain fastness, then You hid your face and I was put to confusion" (Ps. 30:8). The confusion lies in our efforts to keep trying to meditate. Even though our soul would be happy to just remain quiet, something makes us think that we can't live without making our meditation. It is a true moment of purification. "If there is no one to understand these persons (at this stage), they either turn back and abandon the road or lose courage, or at least they hinder their own progress because of their excessive diligence in treading the path of discursive meditation."

A spiritual director who has experience with the path of contemplation will be of great assistance to them. A spiritual director who lacks this experience and tries to keep hammering out their efforts to meditate will only do further harm to their soul. In *The Living Flame of Love,* St. John issues a long and harsh warning to spiritual directors in stanza 3 (par. 30–62). It would prove to be an edifying read for anyone to whom the care of souls has been entrusted. These few excerpts will certainly convey the general message that is relevant here:

How often is God anointing a contemplative with some very delicate unguent of loving knowledge, serene, peaceful, solitary, and far withdrawn from the senses and what is imaginable, as a result of which this person cannot meditate, nor reflect on anything, nor enjoy anything heavenly or earthly (since God has engaged him in that lonely idleness and given him the inclination to solitude), when a spiritual director will happen along who, like a blacksmith, knows no more than how to hammer and pound with the faculties. Since hammering with the faculties is this director's only teaching, and he knows no more than how to meditate, he will say: "Come, now, lay aside these rest periods, which amount to idleness and a waste of time; take and meditate and make interior acts, for it is necessary that you do your part; this other method is the way of illusions and typical of fools."[137]

These spiritual directors, not understanding souls that tread the path of quiet and solitary contemplation, since they themselves have not reached it and do not know what it is to part with discursive meditation, think these souls are idle. They hinder them and hamper the peace of restful and quiet contemplation, which God of His own was according them, by making them walk along the path of meditation and imaginative reflection and perform interior acts. In doing this, these souls find great repugnance, dryness, and distraction; they would want to remain in their holy idleness and quiet and peaceful recollection.... These directors do

[137] St. John of the Cross, *The Living Flame of Love*, 3.43.

> them serious harm, as I said, bringing them grief and ruin, for on the one hand such persons lose ground, and on the other hand they suffer a useless affliction.[138]
>
> These directors do not want the soul to rest and remain quiet, but want it always to labor and work, so that consequently it does not allow room for God's work and ruins and effaces through its own activity what He is doing.[139]

The point St. John is desperately trying to make is that at this stage of the spiritual life, "it is useless for the soul to try and meditate, because it will no longer profit by this exercise." "Meditation is now useless for them, because God is conducting them along another road, which is contemplation."

"The attitude necessary in the night of sense is to pay no attention to discursive meditation, since this is not the time for it. We should allow the soul to remain in rest and quietude, even though it may seem very obvious to us that we are doing nothing and wasting time." "We must be content simply with a loving and peaceful attentiveness to God, and live without the concern, without the effort, and without the desire to taste or feel Him."

St. John's warning to spiritual directors is well taken. And "if there is no one to understand these persons (at this stage)," let us be reassured by the wisdom of St. Teresa in the fourth dwelling, "God will teach the soul what it must do at this point." Trust in God is the remedy.

This is easier said than done, but it is possible. "Through patience and perseverance in prayer, we will be doing a great deal without activity on our part." "All that is required of us here is freedom of soul!" We

[138] Ibid., 3.53.
[139] Ibid., 3.55.

need to free ourselves from the concern of what this all looks like. It is time to walk by faith and not by sight (2 Cor. 5:7). What is seen at the level of the senses will look like an utter waste of time. It takes faith to allow God to lead us into His promised rest. Remember, the curse of Psalm 95: "They shall not enter into my rest." If we resist this rest and keep trying to meditate, we will miss the whole purpose of meditation. Meditation is a preparation for contemplation.

St. John uses the example of a model that needs to sit very still as the artist paints or retouches the portrait. "The artist would be unable to finish, and his work would be disturbed" if the model "should move because of a desire to do something." St. Teresa of Calcutta would regularly ask people to "pray that we may not spoil God's work." Well, try your best now not to spoil God's work of contemplation.

Now is the time to allow Jesus to place His yoke upon your shoulders and learn from Him. Allow Him to lead you into the rest He has promised for our soul (Matt. 11:28–30). Try to adapt the attitude that prayer is remaining in His love (John 15:9) and finding our rest in Him. Let us learn to "be still, and know that I am God" (Ps. 46:11).

St. John closes this chapter with the beautiful definition of contemplation we became familiar with in part one: "Contemplation is nothing else than a secret and peaceful and loving inflow of God, which, if not hampered, fires the soul in the spirit of love, as is brought out in the following verse: 'Fired with love's urgent longings.' "

Explains Three Verses of the Stanza

Chapter Eleven of **The Dark Night**, *Book One*

This secret, peaceful, and loving inflow of God will leave our soul "fired with love's urgent longings" so much that it will leave us wondering how it happened! St. Teresa unfolds this reality in a memorable way using the example of a silkworm in the fifth dwelling. The silkworm, which is fat and ugly, weaves a cocoon and dies within, only to come out a little white butterfly. In the same way, the soul will be left in wonder at the transformation that takes place in prayer. We enter a fat, ugly worm, do nothing but rest, and emerge a little white butterfly. This is the great secret of the mystic's fire of love.

It was said of Pope St. John Paul II that he would periodically enter into the chapel throughout the course of his hectic schedule, lay prostrate on the floor, and emerge from a short time in prayer fully rejuvenated. A little white butterfly indeed!

St. John explains how "the fire of love is not commonly felt at the outset."

This is due to one of three obstacles:

- ✠ Impatience: it is not given a chance to take hold.
- ✠ Blockage: some impurity remains in the sensory part of our soul.
- ✠ Unaccommodation: the soul has not yet provided a peaceful place for it.

How important it is to be patient in the midst of this painful dryness; to allow our every attachment to be purified; and strive to prepare a peaceful place for "the soul's most welcome guest."[140]

The soul will soon become aware of "a certain longing for God," "of being attracted by the love of God and enkindled in it, without knowing how or where this attraction and love originates." It certainly isn't coming from our feelings. The appetites of our soul are being gradually changed from the sensory part to spiritual part. The Psalms are full of examples of a soul thirsting for God; "My soul

[140] Sequence of Pentecost as found in the Roman Missal, 3rd ed.

thirsts for the living God" (Ps. 42:3). The soul has seen the annihilation of all that it formerly found satisfaction in, and yet finds itself mysteriously enamored, "fired with love's urgent longings."

This deep longing for God is complemented by a sincere grief or fear about not serving Him. "This is the sacrifice most pleasing to God — that of a spirit in distress and solicitude for His love."

St. Teresa of Calcutta was indeed a soul "in distress and solicitude for His love." She reveals how "He has destroyed everything in me."[141] "Yet deep down somewhere in my heart that longing for God keeps breaking through the darkness … I find myself telling Jesus unconsciously most strange tokens of love."[142] Indeed, her deep longing for Jesus was "the sacrifice most pleasing to God."

The soul is in the process of undergoing a cure — a cure of self-love. It is through this purging agony that "the soul is being relieved of numerous imperfections and acquires many virtues." These purgations are the path to receiving the grace of healing we long for, as is reflected in this next verse: "Ah, the sheer grace!"

It is *sheer grace* to have passed through this night of purgation. The benefits obtained in this dark night may not seem apparent at the onset, but through this purification of our senses God is uniting the lower part of our soul to the higher part of our soul. The benefits of this dark night will be described in more detail in the next chapter. St. John believes they are all included within this next verse: "I went out unseen."

We had been previously very visible in our spiritual journey, stumbling through all the spiritual imperfections of the seven capital vices. It is true that other people normally see our imperfections much better than we do. Now we go out unseen.

[141] St. Teresa of Calcutta, *Come Be My Light*, 191.
[142] Ibid., 211.

This way that seems "so rough and adverse and contrary to spiritual gratification engenders so many blessings." We are beginning to grow in true love of God. In this night we "have died" to the demands of our senses, "and our life is now hidden with Christ in God" (Col. 3:3). What a blessing it is to be hidden in Him when our only concern is to be pleasing in God's sight — to be freed from the concern of how others might see us.

St. John acknowledges that very few pass through this small gate, this rough and narrow road that leads to life (see Matt. 7:14). To pass through this gate, we need to cease being guided by the gratification of our senses so that we can walk by faith (see 2 Cor. 5:7).

Walking by faith is the aim of the second night. St. John now briefly addresses the second night by observing how the soul will "journey to God in pure faith, for pure faith is the means whereby it is united with God." He remarks how "few walk along this road, because it is so narrow, dark and terrible." The trials of this second night are beyond compare to the first night of senses. The benefits are also incomparably greater.

For now, "we shall say something about the benefits of the night of sense."

The Benefits This Night Causes in the Soul

Chapter Twelve of **The Dark Night**, *Book One*

It is perhaps not possible to overemphasize the spiritual benefits that are gained through this *dark night of the senses,* as it seems we are being deprived of every favor. St. John compares the benefits of this night to that of the great feast Abraham celebrated on the day of his son Isaac's weaning (Gen. 21:8). Abraham rejoiced that his son was going to become a man. In the same manner, there is great rejoicing in Heaven now that God has "taken from this soul its swaddling clothes; that He has put it down from His arms and is making it walk alone; that He is weaning it from the delicate and sweet food of infants and making it eat bread with crust; and that the soul is beginning to taste the food of the strong (the infused contemplation of which we have spoken)."

Heaven knows the great benefits that lie ahead for the weaned children of God.

St. John describes for us the two primary benefits.

1) Knowledge of Self and One's Own Misery

To become aware of one's own misery might not sound like such a great benefit, but it is. God only esteems a soul that is humbled before Him; "A humble, contrite heart you will not spurn" (Ps. 51:19).

Our misery was not so apparent in former times of spiritual consolations. We were content to believe that we were serving God in some way and found satisfaction in our spiritual exercises. We were certainly not convinced of the truth of which Christ tried to persuade us in realizing that we are useless servants (Luke 17:10).

St. John likens this first benefit to that of the Israelites, who were ordered in the book of Exodus to take off their festive ornaments and put on common working clothes, to be aware of the treatment they deserve (Exod. 33:5). It is in our garments of labor, clothed in dryness and desolation, that we now see things more clearly, that we are nothing without God, that "we have [only] done what we were obliged to do" (Luke 17:10).

Now "a person communes with God more respectfully and courteously, the way one should always converse with the *Most High*." No more shaking of statues, as our good sister in the first dwelling was tempted to do. The beginner was more daring with God than was proper. St. John likens this to Moses, who was told to take off his shoes as he hastily approached the burning bush (Exod. 3:4–5). Moses then became so humbled that he hardly dared look up. Similarly, Job's countless blessings did not merit him an intimate conversation with God. Job was quite literally humbled to the ground, naked and on a dunghill, when God was "pleased to descend and speak to him face to face, revealing the deep mysteries of His wisdom, which He never did in the time of Job's prosperity."

It is by descending in knowledge of self that we might ascend to an intimate knowledge of God. This brings us to the second great benefit of this dark night of the senses:

2) Knowledge of God's Grandeur and Majesty

It is not by spiritual delights and gratifications that we are led to an intimate knowledge of God, but rather through the purging of our senses. "In a desert land, without water, dry and without a way, I appeared before you to be able to see your power and your glory" (Ps. 63:2–3).

In order to see God for who He is, I must first recognize who I truly am. In the words of St. Augustine, "Let me know myself Lord, and I will know you."[143]

The philosophers teach us that one extreme is clearly known from the other. Our Lord lovingly instructed St. Catherine of Siena: "Do you know, daughter, who you are and who I am? If you know these two things, you will be blessed. You are she who is not, whereas I am He who is. Have this knowledge in your soul and the enemy will never deceive you."[144]

On Ash Wednesday, one of the options for the words spoken as we are signed with the cross in ashes is "Remember that you are dust, and to dust you shall return." For some reason I had always heard it as "Remember that you *were* dust." But that is not what it says. It is a clear reminder

[143] St. Augustine, As quoted by St. John of the Cross in this chapter with reference to: Solioq., lib.2, c.1-PL 32, 885.

[144] Raymond of Capua, *Life of Catherine of Siena,* trans. and intro. Conleth Kearns, O.P. (Wilmington, Delaware: Michael Glazier, 1980), section 92, p. 85.

that you *are* dust. How strange it is that we often look at others and consider whether this pile of dust is more special than that pile of dust. We are all dust. We are dust through which the very breath of God is presently breathing, giving us His own life, making us much more than dust. If He stops breathing for a millisecond, right back to dust!

These two main benefits — knowledge of self and one's own misery and knowledge of God's grandeur and majesty — go hand in hand. One without the other would prove to be no benefit at all.

To be merely aware of one's own misery could lead to despair, though knowledge of God's grandeur on its own might be an opportunity for presumption.

Through the night of the senses, knowledge of self and one's own misery will ground us in the virtue of humility, while knowledge of God's grandeur and majesty inspires in us the virtue of magnanimity.

Joined properly together, these two virtues bear forth the theological virtue of hope.

Josef Pieper, a renowned expert on St. Thomas Aquinas, describes humility as "the knowledge and acceptance of the inexpressible distance between Creator and creature,"[145] and magnanimity as "the aspiration of the spirit to great things."[146] Pieper goes on to observe that "magnanimity directs us to our true possibilities, while humility with its gaze fixed on the infinite distance between man and God, reveals the limitations of these possibilities and preserves them from sham realization and for true realization."[147]

It would be a sham to think we could be united with God through our own meager efforts.

[145] Josef Pieper, *On Hope* (San Francisco: Ignatius Press, 1986), 29.
[146] Ibid., 28
[147] Ibid., 29.

In the Blessed Virgin Mary, we encounter a profound example of how the virtues of humility and magnanimity are able to preserve in us the true realization of hope. At a tender age she openly recognized her own lowliness (humility) and remained open to the truly wonderful works of God (magnanimity). These two virtues were beautifully expressed in her acknowledgment: "He has looked with favor on His lowly servant [humility], from this day all generations will call me blessed [magnanimity]" (Luke 1:48). Through the beautiful union of these two virtues, Mary became the mother of "our life, our sweetness, and our hope."[148]

In the Church's wisdom, we are directed at every Mass to exercise both humility and magnanimity as we prepare for our great hope of communing with Jesus. We pray: "Lord, I am not worthy that you should enter under my roof [humility], but only say the word and my soul shall be healed [magnanimity]."

Through this night of the senses, the beautiful hope Jesus prayed for, that "they may all be one, as you, Father, are in me and I in you, that they also may be in us" (John 17:21), is precisely what is unfolding.

For this to happen, we first need to realize that we are dust. Then in the dusty haze of humility, an authentic knowledge of God begins to settle in, opening the way for His mighty light to shine forth through the darkness of our soul and guide us into His promised rest.

One of the main benefits of this dark night of the senses is the spiritual humility that serves to purify us of the spiritual imperfection of pride. St. John concludes this chapter by explaining that "the thought of being more advanced than others does not even occur in our mind as it did before." We are now too busy with our own faults to be scrutinizing those of others. With no time left for judging others, we

[148] From the prayer, *Hail, Holy Queen (Salve Regina).*

might decide to love our neighbor, and maybe even be open to learning something from them. "Since we are so aware of our own wretchedness, we not only listen to the teaching of others, but even desire to be directed and told what to do by anyone at all."

Other Benefits of This Dark Night of Senses

Chapter Thirteen of **The Dark Night**, *Book One*

St. John may have been getting ahead of himself in addressing the spiritual imperfection of pride while still in the previous chapter. In this present chapter he will describe the benefits of how all the remaining spiritual imperfections of the seven capital sins identified at the beginning of his book are being purified through the dark night of the senses. His anticipation for moving on to the *dark night of the spirit* becomes very evident from his remarks on the benefit of being freed from the "innumerable" spiritual imperfections of gluttony. He bluntly states: "I will not refer to them here, since I am anxious to conclude this dark night in order to pass on to the important doctrine we have concerning the other night."

The benefits he describes in this chapter are worth going through in brief detail. I have found it helpful to organize them into a threefold hierarchy of benefits.

First, all of the spiritual imperfections of the remaining capital sins receive a thorough house cleaning through this night of the senses.

Then, since there is no more effective cleansing agent of vice than virtue, the soul now enjoys a much more virtuous home.

Finally, in the home of this virtuous soul, God will prove to be "the soul's most welcome guest"[149] by making more frequent visits.

Now, these benefits in detail:

[149] Sequence of Pentecost as found in the Roman Missal, 3rd ed.

In regard to spiritual avarice, spiritual lust, and spiritual gluttony, "God so curbs concupiscence and bridles the appetite through this arid and dark night that the soul cannot feast on any sensory delight from earthly or heavenly things." We find it much easier to resist greed, lust, and gluttony when there is no longer any pleasure to be found in what caused us to be greedy, lustful, and gluttonous.

Spiritual avarice "undergoes a thorough reform" since the delight the soul formerly found in coveting objects, and that drove it to extremes in spiritual exercises, has been moderated. "They become detached from many things because of this lack of gratification."

Spiritual lust loses its grip on the soul. "Through the sensory dryness and distaste experienced in its spiritual exercises, the soul is freed of those impurities we noted."

As for spiritual gluttony, "let it suffice to say that the soul is liberated from all the imperfections we mentioned and from many other greater evils and foul abominations, not listed, into which many have fallen, as we know from experience, because they did not reform their desire for this spiritual sweetness."

God knows what He is doing in this dark night: "The passions, as a result, lose their strength and become sterile from not receiving any satisfaction, just as the courses of the udder dry up when milk is not drawn through them daily." "Once the soul's appetites have withered, and it lives in spiritual sobriety, admirable benefits result."

As for the spiritual imperfections of the three remaining vices of anger, envy, and sloth, the soul has been softened and humbled by the hardships, temptations, and trials through which it has passed in the course of this night. The result is a spiritual meekness toward God, ourselves, and our neighbor.

Spiritual anger no longer impatiently arises at the sight of faults — our own or those of our neighbor. The temptation to become displeased with ourselves or disrespectfully querulous (full of complaints) with God for not making us perfect more quickly is now abated.

Spiritual envy is subdued by an utter awareness of our own misery. We are now much more willing to concede the goodness of others. The envy that remains is a holy envy of wanting to imitate the virtues of others.

Spiritual sloth is not as alluring as before. We now have the training and stamina to walk this rough way, knowing more firmly that it does lead to the rest we so desire.

In the midst of this purification, "God frequently communicates to the soul, when it least expects, a spiritual sweetness, a very pure love, and a spiritual knowledge which is sometimes most delicate." The soul realizes that these touches of God are much more precious than all that was previously sought. Our love for God is no longer motivated by delights, consolations, and gratifications. With a purer love for God in our heart, "the soul bears a habitual remembrance of God, accompanied by a fear and dread of turning back on the spiritual road."

"Another very great benefit for the soul in this night is that it exercises all the virtues together." The theological and cardinal virtues are now working together in aiding us to carry out the spiritual and corporal works of mercy.

We are now more freed from the hands of our enemies: the world, the flesh, and the devil. These are the foes St. John identifies in their efforts to keep us living at the level of our senses, seeking gratification.

The four passions — joy, sorrow, hope, and fear — on which we formerly rode the roller coaster of life with its highs and lows, are now calmed through the constant practice of mortification.

With all our natural appetites of the senses lulled to sleep, the soul now says of its lower part, "My house being now all stilled."

An Explanation of the Last Verse of the First Stanza

Chapter Fourteen of The Dark Night, *Book One*

Our house, composed of its senses, is now all stilled. Through the trials of this dark night our passions have been quenched, our appetites calmed and put to sleep. Our soul can now journey along the road of the spirit. On this path, often referred to as the illuminative way or infused contemplation, "God Himself pastures and refreshes the soul without any of its own discursive meditation or active help."

To those God wills to bring through the second *night of the spirit,* the need to strengthen them for the road ahead is realized through the storms and trials He sends into the sensory night. The spirit of fornication can come to afflict the soul with foul thoughts and very vivid images, which can sometimes prove to be a pain worse than death. At other times a blasphemous spirit is added, which comes so strongly to the imagination that a soul is almost made to pronounce them. This grave torment is evident in the writings of St. Teresa of Calcutta, who revealed, "In my soul I feel just that terrible pain of loss — of God not wanting me — of God not being God — of God not really existing (Jesus please forgive my blasphemies — I have been told to write everything)."[150] Then sometimes a loathsome spirit, which Isaiah calls *spiritus vertiginis* ("spirit of dizziness"; Isa. 19:14), is sent to fill one with a thousand scruples and perplexities. This can so mess with our mind that our

[150] St. Teresa of Calcutta, *Come Be My Light,* 192–193.

judgment seems to never be content or comforted, even by the good counsel of others. "This is one of the most burdensome goads and horrors of this night — very similar to what occurs in the spiritual night." It is what will eventually enable us to "walk by faith, not by sight" (2 Cor. 5:7), not forming our judgments by what we see or perceive others to see, but by what we have come to believe by faith that God sees.

There is no textbook case of the dark night of the senses. God will guide each soul in the way that is best for it to be purified and raised to the degree of love He has planned for it. "Those who have considerably more capacity and strength for suffering, God purges more intensely and quickly." The natural sufferings of our former life become a type of "Oh happy fault,"[151] as they will have conditioned us to persevere in the midst of such trials.

"Those who are very weak He keeps in this night for a long time. Their purgation is less intense and their temptations abated." "God frequently refreshes their senses to keep them from backsliding. They arrive at the purity of perfection later in life. And some of them will never reach it entirely, for they are never wholly in or wholly out of the night." Realizing what is best for their soul, God sees that they might lose courage and return to their search for consolation in the things of this world. He comes to their aid with His consolation when it is needed, while trying to exercise them in humility and self-knowledge through the trials they are able to endure.

That concludes the first night of the senses. Many of us have likely experienced some of what has been covered.

Let us recall St. John's purpose for writing what he did on this night:

[151] From the Easter Exsultet proclaimed on the Easter Vigil as found in the Roman Missal, 3rd ed.

- ✠ To help beginners understand the feebleness of their state
- ✠ To give them courage
- ✠ To give them the desire for God to place them in this night

We can only pray that it has done just that. I have found that it also serves to authenticate our experience, helps us understand the ongoing purification, and can enable us to assist others to recognize God's purifying hand in their own soul. Hopefully, it inspires one to read further about the second night of the spirit.

For the moment, let us return to the fifth dwelling of St. Teresa's *Interior Castle,* with which part two of this book will conclude.

CHAPTER 9

THE INTERIOR CASTLE:

THE FIFTH DWELLING PLACE

FLYING FREE FROM OUR ATTACHMENTS

"IF SOULS DO no more than reach the door, God is being very merciful to them; although many are called few are chosen." St. Teresa sadly observes that few people dispose themselves to the Lord's way of communicating, even those who have been called to a contemplative vocation.

In *The Ascent of Mount Carmel,* St. John of the Cross stresses that the disposition needed in prayer to be led by God into His promised rest entails our "being freed from every appetite, however slight."[152] He reasons that "it makes little difference whether a bird is tied by a thin thread or by a cord. For even if tied by a thread, the bird will be prevented from taking off just as surely as if it were tied by a cord."[153]

This point is reminiscent of the one we drew upon earlier from *The Living Flame of Love,* where St. John demonstrated how our attachments are what keep us from swimming in the unctions of God.[154]

[152] St. John of the Cross, *The Collected Works of St. John of the Cross, The Ascent of Mount Carmel,* 1.11.3.

[153] Ibid., 1.11.4.

[154] St. John of the Cross, *The Living Flame of Love,* 3.64.

What keeps us from flying free and swimming in the unctions of God are all the attachments the dark night is trying to purify in us. A good list of some of those attachments is found in the Litany of Humility.[155] (See appendix B for this prayer in its entirety.) This litany can serve as a type of litmus test for showing us where our heart is attached to something other than God. It will help us to recognize what is keeping us from flying free and swimming in the unctions of God. We need to be freed from our attachment to the desires of being loved, extolled, honored, praised, preferred, consulted, approved, and popular. We need to be delivered from the fears of being humiliated, despised, rebuked, calumniated, forgotten, wronged, ridiculed, and suspected. Through this litany we are guided to pray for the grace to desire that others be loved more than us; esteemed more than us; to be freed from worrying about the opinion of the world; and like St. John the Baptist, to desire others to increase and for us to decrease (John 3:30). The Litany of Humility is a true prayer of deliverance to keep our heart free from the disturbances the enemy likes to stir in our souls when others are chosen and I set aside; when they are praised and I left unnoticed; when they are preferred to me in everything. Finally, we are guided to the noble desire for others to become holier than I, provided that I become as holy as I should.

St. John remarks, "It is a matter of deep sorrow that while God had bestowed upon them the power to break with other stronger cords of attachments, they fail to attain so much good because they do not become detached from some childish thing which God has requested them to conquer out of love for Him."[156] "It is regrettable, then to behold some souls, laden as rich vessels with wealth, deeds,

[155] Litany of Humility, as composed by Rafael Cardinal Merry del Val, secretary of state to Pope St. Pius X.

[156] St. John of the Cross, *The Ascent of Mount Carmel,* 1.11.5.

spiritual exercises, virtues, and favors from God, never advancing because they lack the courage to make a complete break with some little satisfaction, attachment, or affection (which are all about the same), and thereby never reaching the port of perfection, which requires no more than a sudden flap of one's wings to tear the thread of attachment."[157]

What St. John is saying is so true. Think of all the things we have already renounced for the sake of following Jesus. Then consider those little things we keep holding onto that keep us from flying free and swimming in His unctions.

The whole matter of detachment can at times tempt us to throw up our hands and contend that contemplation is simply not for us. How can we not have attachments to our loved ones, particularly those called to the state of marriage in which they have a spouse and children? It is true that thoughts and concerns of our loved ones will enter our time of prayer. It is precisely there that we are called to entrust them to the Lord. If we do not entrust them to the Lord, then our attachment to them will keep us from flying free and swimming in His unctions. Detachment requires us to recognize that not even our children are truly our own. They are the Lord's, entrusted to our good keeping, but only for a time. This doesn't mean that we don't love them and care for them. It does mean, however, that "whoever loves father or mother more than me is not worthy of me, and whoever loves son or daughter more than me is not worthy of me" (Matt. 10:37). Our care for those entrusted to us is a service to God. In this service we must remain mindful of keeping God first. We can have no other gods before Him.

The traditional line drawn between Martha and Mary, with Mary standing out as the contemplative model, may be helpful here.

[157] Ibid., 1.11.4.

In making His memorable comment to Martha, Jesus wasn't telling her to stop preparing the meal. It was quite likely God's will for her in that moment. Everyone would have gone hungry that night had Martha quit serving. What Jesus was trying to do was set her heart free from the attachment of being "worried and anxious about many things" (Luke 10:41), especially distress over her sister, Mary. Worldly anxieties are the thorns Jesus identifies as choking off the seed of His word from bearing fruit (Matt. 13:22). To fly free and swim in the unctions of God, all of these concerns, worries, and anxieties over our loved ones must be entrusted to Him. There is indeed only "one thing necessary" (Luke 10:42). To attend to that one thing requires a detachment from everything else.

Few people are willing to do that in prayer. They choose, instead, to spend much of their time in prayer "burdened with much serving" (Luke 10:40). The servant who wants to fly free and swim in the unctions of God must learn how to take His yoke upon his shoulders, and find his rest in Him. Entering into His rest is the pearl of great price for which we must be willing to sell everything (Matt. 13:46). St. Teresa observes that this is not a treasure for which we need to dig; this "treasure lies within our very selves."

The beauty of entering into His rest is unfolding for the soul in this fifth dwelling. This restful state of union described by St. Teresa is not a "dreamy state." It "only seems that the soul is asleep." We cannot bring about this state of rest on our own. There is no technique we can use "to suspend the mind, since all the faculties are asleep in this state — and truly asleep — to the things of the world and to ourselves." "During the time this union lasts, the soul is left as though without its senses; for it has no power to think even if it wants to." We become "like one who in every respect has died to the world so as to live more completely in God."

The Experience of Union Colored by Doubt

Even though this experience is profound, the soul will remain doubtful whether it was truly one with God. We will find ourselves considering whether that experience was real or just imagined. Was I sleeping? Have I succumbed to spiritual sloth? Was this from God, or did the devil transform himself into an angel of light? "We are left with a thousand suspicions."

The Enemy

"If the prayer is truly that of union with God, the devil cannot enter to do damage. His Majesty is so joined and united with the essence of the soul that the devil will not dare approach nor will he even know about this secret." The devil is unaware of what is happening; he is unable to see such a pure communication of love. It is unlike the efforts we make in meditation when he can see what passes through our imagination. Since God's gift of contemplation does not enter through the mind "the soul is left with such wonderful blessings because God works within it without anyone disturbing Him, not even ourselves!" "During the time of union the soul neither sees, nor hears, nor understands, because the union is always short and seems to the soul even much shorter than it probably is."

Certitude of Experience

If the experience is authentic, "God so places Himself in the interior part of the soul that when it returns to itself it can in no way doubt that it was in God and God was in it. This truth remains so firmly that even though years go by without God's granting that favor again, the soul can neither forget nor doubt that it was in God and God was in it."

St. Teresa's words bring us back to Jesus' prayer that "they may all be one, as you, Father, are in me and I in you, that they also may be in us" (John 17:21), that "the love with which you loved me may be in them and I in them" (v. 26). This prayer is now being fulfilled. This is something that can really happen! When it does truly happen, God gives our soul the certitude that "it was in God and God was in it." "Whoever does not receive this certitude does not experience union of the whole soul with God, but union of some faculty, or that he experiences one of the many other kinds of favors God grants souls."

In this prayer of union, God does not enter through the intellect, memory, or will. "He wants to enter the center of the soul without going through any door, as He entered the place where His disciples were (after the resurrection) when He said, '*pax vobis*' (peace be with you)" (John 20:19).

The Example of a Silkworm

St. Teresa now unfolds her memorable example of a silkworm to demonstrate the transformation that can take place in a soul when it is properly disposed for prayer.

A silkworm begins as a very small cell, develops into a worm with warm weather, and nourishes itself on twigs of mulberry trees. It then spins a cocoon of silk into which it is enclosed. "The silkworm, which is fat and ugly, then dies, and a little white butterfly, which is very pretty, comes forth from the cocoon."

In a similar fashion, the soul now begins to live by the warmth of the Holy Spirit through the remedies of the Church: going to Confession, reading good books, and hearing sermons. One starts to live by these things and by their good meditations. One continues to grow and begin to spin the silk of the house in which they will eventually die. This death to self comes about "by getting rid of self-love and self-will, our attachment to any earthly thing, and by performing deeds of penance, prayer, mortification and obedience." Then, "when the soul is truly dead to the world in this prayer of union, a little white butterfly comes forth. Oh the greatness of God!" The soul that comes forth from this prayer of union is transformed!

The soul emerges from this time of prayer and doesn't even recognize itself. It was an ugly worm when it entered. The soul wonders at the transformation. It knows that it didn't merit this blessing. St. Teresa excitedly remarks, "How transformed the soul is when it comes out of this prayer after having been placed within the greatness of God and so closely joined with Him for a little while."

One emerges from this short time in prayer of union, which in Teresa's opinion "never lasts for as much as a half hour," with a desire to praise God and to make Him known.

Effects

"Oh, now the restlessness of this little butterfly, even though it has never been quieter and calmer in its life, is something to praise God for!" "Since it has experienced such wonderful rest, all that it sees on earth displeases it." "It no longer has any esteem for the works it did while a worm." "Everything it can do for God becomes little in its own eyes." "It now has wings. How can it be happy walking step-by-step when it can fly?"

New trials arise for the soul that has been nourished by this heavenly food. Worldly things no longer hold any pleasure for it. "There is a painful desire to leave this world. Any relief the soul has, comes from the thought that God wants it to be living in this exile." The desire to leave this world reveals that "in spite of all these benefits, it (the soul) is not entirely surrendered to God's will." It is much more willing to conform to His will, "but it conforms with a great feeling that it can do no more because no more has been given it, and with many tears."

What St. Teresa describes here reflects what was learned from St. John about the benefits of the dark night of the senses. The soul has now gained some "knowledge of God's grandeur and majesty."[158] This knowledge is so beyond anything they have ever experienced that they desire to praise God in a way that is beyond what is possible. St. Teresa of Calcutta would express her "longing to love Jesus as He had never been loved before." It is a cause of deep pain to not be able to praise and love God to the degree of our desire. That other main benefit of the dark night of the senses, "knowledge of self and one's own misery,"[159] stands before us with clarity.

Added to this is "the deep pain it feels at seeing that God is offended and little esteemed in this world and that many souls are lost." "Even though it sees that God's mercy is great — it fears that many are being condemned." St. Teresa gives praise to God for a soul to experience such pain. "A few years ago, and even perhaps days — this soul wasn't mindful of anything but itself. Who has placed it in the midst of such painful concerns? Even were we to meditate for many years, we wouldn't be able to feel them as painfully as does this soul now." In his encyclical letter, *Deus caritas est,* Pope Benedict XVI explains, "God's will is no longer for me an alien will, something imposed on me from without by the commandments, but it is now my own will."[160] He draws upon an ancient quote on love in Latin that quite beautifully expresses this union of wills, *idem velle atque idem nolle*[161] (to want the same thing and to reject the same thing). As St. Teresa explains, "Its great love makes it so surrendered that it neither knows nor wants anything more than what He wants."

In this prayer of union, God impresses His seal upon our soul. The soul has become like wax in its surrender to God. St. Teresa

[158] St. John of the Cross, *The Dark Night,* 1.12.4.

[159] Ibid., 1.12.2.

[160] Benedict XVI, Encyclical Letter *Deus caritas est* (Vatican City: Libreria Editrice Vaticana, 2006), par. 17.

[161] Sallust, *De coniuratione Catilinae,* 20, 4, in *Deus caritas est,* par. 17.

observes that we "go forth from this union impressed with His seal," without understanding how it happened. For "the wax doesn't impress the seal upon itself; it is only disposed — by remaining still and giving its consent." "The soul does no more in this union than does wax when another impresses a seal upon it."

It is very similar to the seal impressed upon us at the very moment of our creation, when through no merit of our own or hindrance of any attachment that would separate us from the will of God; God "set His seal upon us" (2 Cor. 1:22). Pope Benedict XVI borrows an analogy from biology in remarking that it is as if God's seal is imprinted upon our genome (the entire set of an organism's hereditary information). So much does "the human being [bear] the profound mark of the Trinity, of God as Love."[162]

Catching Fire from Fire

With His seal set upon us, we go forward in service of Our Lord in true self-knowledge. We recognize along with St. Paul that "it is no longer I who live, but Christ who lives in me" (Gal. 2:20). Being "fired with love's urgent longings,"[163] many beautiful benefits are brought to other souls as "they catch fire from its fire." Even when the soul is not experiencing the fire of this union, "the inclination to benefit others will remain, and the soul delights in explaining the favors God grants to whoever loves and serves Him."

Union of Wills

"True union can very well be reached, with God's help, if we make the effort to obtain it by keeping our wills fixed only on that which is God's will." We need to be firm in our resolve to do only the will

[162] Benedict XVI, Angelus (June 7, 2009).
[163] St. John of the Cross, *The Dark Night*, 1.10.6.

of God. "Oh, how desirable is this union with God's will! Happy the soul that has reached it." The soul in union with the will of God "lives tranquilly in this life, and in the next as well." The only thing that afflicts it is when it sees God offended or is placed in some danger of losing God. St. Teresa notes that this doesn't make us immune to the sufferings produced by our human nature. We don't become stoical (unfeeling). The death of a family member is still felt and there will remain trials and sicknesses that aren't always suffered happily. The four passions St. John spoke of — joy, sorrow, hope, and fear — will remain. However, we no longer allow them to take us on the roller coaster ride of exhilarating highs and devastating lows.

In my second year of being a priest, my bishop forwarded two letters that were sent to him concerning me. One was filled with praise, the other with condemnation. He accompanied the letters with the wise advice of a baseball coach to his players: "Don't get too high when you are winning or too low when you are losing. It is a long season."

We too are on a long pilgrimage. If we "deny [ourselves], pick up [our] cross daily and follow me" (Luke 9:23), then "even though [we] walk through a dark valley, [we] fear no evil for you are at [our] side" (Ps. 23:4).

Humble Self-knowledge Is the Battle

St. Teresa observes that in this dwelling "great are the wiles of the devil; to make us think we have one virtue — when we don't — he would circle hell a thousand times." We can sometimes be certain in prayer that we are ready to be humiliated and publicly insulted for God. Then, afterwards, we might try to hide even a tiny fault if we could; "or, if they have not committed one and yet are charged with it — God deliver us!"

The one area that warrants our careful attention is love for neighbor. We can "be certain that the more advanced you see you are in love for your neighbor, the more advanced you will be in love of God." For "we cannot know whether or not we love God, although there are strong indications for recognizing that we do love Him: but we can know whether we love our neighbor."

Betrothal on the Way

The prayer of union that St. Teresa has been describing for us in this fifth dwelling "does not yet reach the stage of spiritual betrothal." Just like in an earthly engagement, all the arrows are pointing toward marriage, but the marriage has not yet taken place. She warns us to take great care to not place our affection in something other than God and promptly remove ourselves from such occasions. "If we are careless about placing our affection in something other than Him, we lose everything."

The betrothal is coming, but the soul is not yet entirely surrendered to God. The enemy knows this and "will go about very carefully in order to fight against and prevent this betrothal. Afterward, since he sees the soul entirely surrendered to the Spouse, he doesn't dare do so much, because he fears it." At the stage of betrothal the enemy would gather all of Hell together for the purpose of deterring such a soul, for a multitude of souls is at stake. Teresa points to the examples of St. Dominic and St. Francis, whose lives served to impact numerous souls. In our own day it is easy to identify the profound impact St. Teresa of Calcutta and Pope St. John Paul II have had, and are still having, upon the lives of many others.

The Enemy

We might ask ourselves, how can such a soul be deceived, since it doesn't want to do anything but God's will in everything? "What are the ways in which the devil can enter so dangerously that your soul goes astray?"

At this stage the devil realizes that he is not going to tempt us with evil, so he shifts his efforts toward trying to keep our will from being united to the will of God. He "comes along with some skillful deception and, under the color of good, confuses it with regard to little things and induces it to get taken up with some of them that he makes it think are good. Then little by little he darkens the intellect, cools the will's ardor, and makes self-love grow until in one way or another he withdraws the soul from the will of God and brings it to his own."

It takes great patience to carefully discern the will of God. We can still be fooled by our feelings and emotions and fail to wait for God's still, small voice. In St. Teresa's telling words, "We love ourselves very much."

While I was living as a hermit, as a fruit of this vocation to prayerful solitude, I would give a few retreats each year to the Missionaries of Charity. The first year God had something to teach me about the need to carefully discern His will. I had begun living as a hermit in July and a retreat was scheduled for February in Albania. A few months prior to the retreat, they called to ask if I could give an additional retreat in Rome before I returned to the United States. I rather hastily agreed. My spiritual director was in Rome, so I welcomed the opportunity to pay him a visit and was ready for a diversion from solitude. At the end of the first retreat, the Lord made it very evident in my heart that this had not been a proper discernment. Each retreat is nine days long. With travel time, it was going to work out to over three weeks away from the life of solitude. The wisdom of the first hermit, St. Anthony of the Desert, was being impressed upon me: "Just as fish die if they stay too long out of water, so the monks who loiter outside their cells or pass their time with men of the world lose the intensity of inner peace. So like a fish going towards the sea, we must hurry to reach our cell, for fear that if we delay outside we will lose our interior watchfulness."[164]

On our way to the airport in Albania to catch the flight to Rome, the regional superior asked if I would be willing to come back next year to give a retreat there and another one in Naples. In my heart, I knew that I could not do two retreats in a row again. As I began to relate this to her, she told me not to give an answer right now, but to pray about it.

When I arrived in Rome, who was there to greet me but the regional superior of Naples. During my years as a seminarian in Rome, she had become a dear friend of mine through her sound spiritual counsel and inspiring example. It was a great joy to see her again. She was excited to relate the invitation to return next year and give a retreat for her sisters. I told her that I didn't think I could give two retreats in a row again as it would require too lengthy of a departure from my vocation as a hermit. She beckoned me to consider the number of souls this would help. I remarked that many more souls could be aided in a hidden way if I remain true to my vocation as a hermit. She then informed me that this was her final year as regional superior in Naples and that we might not see each other again if I didn't come. As I began to relate to her what the Lord had been putting in my heart, she too asked me not to give an answer now, but to pray about it.

What followed was nearly a month of discernment. I found myself going back and forth, again and again, on this decision. I was truly torn. The reason I relate this story is because the discernment I was faced with was not between something good and something evil. It was between two goods. In my heart of hearts, I sensed what God was asking. He was making it clear that to remain true to my vocation

[164] St. Anthony the Great, *The Sayings of the Desert Fathers*, 3.

as a hermit, only one retreat should be scheduled and that this would preferably be in the United States. How tempting it was to choose my own preference that would enable me to spend some time with this good friend and possibly see my spiritual director again. After a long process of going back and forth on my decision, it was evident that Our Lord wanted me to remain in the hermitage. When I finally related my decision, within the hour I received a call from the Missionaries of Charity in Memphis, Tennessee, asking for a retreat within that same time period. God was so good to immediately confirm that I had made a proper discernment.

All the enemy wants to do is separate us from the will of God, even if for a moment. That is his determined focus at this point, and "there is no enclosure so fenced in that he cannot enter, or desert so withdrawn that he fails to go there."

The Battle

St. Teresa observes that God likely permits such battles to unfold in this fifth dwelling "to observe the behavior of that soul He wishes to set up as a light for others. If there is going to be a downfall, it's better that it happen in the beginning rather than later, when it would be harmful to many." But the devil is not given an easy task; it is not as if "a soul that comes so close to God is allowed to lose Him so quickly." "His Majesty would regret the loss of this soul so much that He gives it in many ways a thousand interior warnings, so that the harm will not be hidden from it."

God will enlighten such a soul to recognize when it has begun to stray. For our part, "we must always ask God in prayer to sustain us." We would be fools to trust our own discernment. We must constantly beg God to show us the way. Then, we must pay close attention to our own practice of virtue, especially in love of neighbor and in performing ordinary daily tasks. St. Teresa of Calcutta gives some shrewd advice on performing these ordinary tasks: "We are at Jesus' disposal. If He wants you sick in bed; if He wants you to proclaim His work in the street; if He wants you to clean the toilets all day; that's all right, everything is all right. We must say, 'I belong to you. You can do whatever you like.' And this is our strength, and this is the joy of the Lord." St. Teresa of Calcutta knew that the holiest thing we can do in any given moment of each day is the will of God. Hers was a soul not easily swayed from the will of God, and one whom the devil certainly came to fear.

St. Teresa of Ávila's final word in this dwelling: "Let this, in sum, be the conclusion: that we strive always to advance. And if we don't advance, let us walk with great fear. Without doubt, the devil wants to cause some lapse."

"Love is never idle, and failure to grow would be a very bad sign."

St. John of the Cross will agree that "not to go forward on this road is to turn back, and not to gain ground is to lose."[165]

[165] St. John of the Cross, *The Ascent of Mount Carmel*, 1.11.5.

Conclusion of Part Two

With those words of St. John of the Cross, we are indeed compelled to go forward to what he was most intent upon sharing in his commentary on *The Dark Night.*

For many years, the material I gave on retreats was only what we covered in part one and part two. I had been asked many times to put that material in a printed form that could be more readily accessible. By the grace of God, this is what you are holding now.

One group of sisters was so engaged by the retreat given on this material that they beckoned me to prepare and present a retreat on the sixth and seventh dwellings of *The Interior Castle* and the second night of the spirit of *The Dark Night.* It is hard to put it exactly into words, but their response made me realize that it might not yet be time to let this "servant go in peace" (Luke 2:29).

The eventual content of part three is what St. John remarked upon earlier: "hardly anything has been said of it, in sermons or in writing, and even the experience of it is rare."[166] This remains true today, five hundred years later.

[166] St. John of the Cross, *The Dark Night,* 1.8.2.

It is worth noting the amount of time St. Teresa and St. John devote to explaining the sixth and seventh dwelling and the second night of the spirit.

- ✠ In *The Interior Castle,* the first five dwellings comprise ninety-five pages.
- ✠ The sixth and seventh dwellings alone have just as many pages.
- ✠ In *The Dark Night,* the first night of the senses is described in thirty-two pages.
- ✠ The second night of the spirit takes twice as long to explain.

This fact alone can help us appreciate that the full scope of their understanding of this journey is necessary for us to appreciate the path by which we can be led into the depth of His rest. It did not require the sisters on that retreat to have a personal experience of all that was being described to be fully engaged by what was being explained and appreciate that this is indeed the path upon which one is led into His rest. Together we observed that what was being described as the process of purification in prayer is what souls often seem to be experiencing in the dying process. In the dying process we eventually need to detach from everything in this world that we find hard to think we can live without. We will be detached from our home, our possessions, our health, our freedom to go where we want, to do what we will, and even our ability to clearly express the desires of our heart and mind.

In his Prayer of Peace, St. Francis observed, "It is in dying that we are born to eternal life." Jesus Himself refers to our time on earth as a period of labor for birth (Matt. 24:8; John 16:21). Ever since our Baptism, we are in the process of being born into eternal life. Eventually in this time of labor, we are detached from all that we thought was needed to live. When a child is born, they are detached from all that gave life to them in the womb. This is necessary so that their eyes can be opened to see, and they take their first breath of air. So, too, will our time of labor on earth necessarily detach us from all that would hinder our eyes from being opened to see what the children of God have been created to see and enable us to take in our initial breath of eternal life.

"And you will find rest" is the journey being described.

Eternal rest is the ultimate place He will lead us.

So, I invite you to pray for me as I go forward in this labor of striving to compose the remaining chapters of *The Interior Castle* and *The Dark Night* in a similar format as you have read in part two.

Appendix A

The Dark Night

1. One dark night,
fired with love's urgent longings
— ah, the sheer grace! —
I went out unseen,
my house being now all stilled.

2. In darkness, and secure,
by the secret ladder, disguised,
— ah, the sheer grace! —
In darkness and concealment,
my house being now all stilled.

3. On that glad night,
in secret, for no one saw me,
nor did I look at anything,
with no other light or guide
than the one that burned in my heart.

4. This guided me
more surely than the light of noon
to where he was awaiting me

—him I knew so well—
there in a place where no one appeared.

5. O guiding night!
O night more lovely than the dawn!
O night that has united
the Lover with his beloved,
transforming the beloved in her Lover.

6. Upon my flowering breast
which I kept wholly for him alone,
there he lay sleeping,
and I caressing him
there in a breeze from the fanning cedars.

7. When the breeze blew from the turret,
as I parted his hair,
it wounded my neck
with its gentle hand,
suspending all my senses.

8. I abandoned and forgot myself,
laying my face on my Beloved;
all things ceased; I went out from myself,
leaving my cares
forgotten among the lilies.

Appendix B

Litany of Humility

O Jesus! Meek and humble of heart, *Hear me.*

From the desire of being esteemed, *Deliver me, Jesus.*
From the desire of being loved, *Deliver me, Jesus.*
From the desire of being extolled, *Deliver me, Jesus.*
From the desire of being honored, *Deliver me, Jesus.*
From the desire of being praised, *Deliver me, Jesus.*
From the desire of being preferred to others, *Deliver me, Jesus.*
From the desire of being consulted, *Deliver me, Jesus.*
From the desire of being approved, *Deliver me, Jesus.*
From the fear of being humiliated, *Deliver me, Jesus.*
From the fear of being despised, *Deliver me, Jesus.*
From the fear of suffering rebukes, *Deliver me, Jesus.*
From the fear of being calumniated, *Deliver me, Jesus.*
From the fear of being forgotten, *Deliver me, Jesus.*
From the fear of being ridiculed, *Deliver me, Jesus.*
From the fear of being wronged, *Deliver me, Jesus.*
From the fear of being suspected, *Deliver me, Jesus.*

That others may be loved more than I,
Jesus, grant me the grace to desire it.
That others may be esteemed more than I,
Jesus, grant me the grace to desire it.
That, in the opinion of the world, others may increase and I may decrease,
Jesus, grant me the grace to desire it.
That others may be chosen and I set aside,
Jesus, grant me the grace to desire it.
That others may be praised and I unnoticed,
Jesus, grant me the grace to desire it.
That others may be preferred to me in everything,
Jesus, grant me the grace to desire it.
That others may become holier than I,
provided that I may become as holy as I should,
Jesus, grant me the grace to desire it.

Bibliography

A Carthusian. *The Call of Silent Love*. London: Darton, Longman and Todd, 1995.

A Carthusian. *The Way of Silent Love*. London: Darton, Longman and Todd, 1994.

A Carthusian. *They Speak by Silences*. London: Darton, Longman and Todd, 1996.

A Monk. *The Hermitage Within*. Translated by Alan Neame. London: Darton, Longman and Todd, 1999.

Anthony the Great, St. *The Sayings of the Desert Fathers*. Translated by Benedicta Ward. Kalamazoo, MI: Cistercian Press, 1984.

Aquinas, St. Thomas. *Summa Theologica*. Translated by Fathers of the English Dominican Province. Westminster, MD: Christian Classics, 1981.

Augustine, St. *Confessions*. Translated by Henry Chadwick. Oxford: Oxford University Press, 1991.

———. *In Iohannis Evangelium Tractatus*. In *Veritatis splendor*. Vatican City: Libreria Editrice Vaticana, 1993.

Benedict XVI. Angelus. August 19, 2007.

———. Angelus. June 7, 2009.

———. *Deus caritas est*. Vatican City: Liberia Editrice Vaticana, 2006.

———. *God and the World: A Conversation with Peter Seewald*. San Francisco: Ignatius Press, 2002.

———. *Introduction to Christianity*. San Francisco: Ignatius Press, 2004.

———. Mass of Inauguration Homily. April 25, 2005.

Bernard of Clairvaux, St. *On the Song of Songs*. Kalamazoo, MI: Cistercian, 1980.

Bosco, St. John. *The Liturgy of the Hours*, vol. 3. New York: Catholic Book Publishing Co., 1975.

Bruno, St. *Letter to Raoul Le Verd*. Translated by A Carthusian. In *The Wound of Love*. London: Darton, Longman and Todd, 1994.

Catechism of the Catholic Church. Saint Paul, MN: The Wanderer Press, 1994.

Catherine of Siena, St. *Letter to Monna Agnese*. Translated by Vida di Scudder. In *Saint Catherine of Siena as Seen in Her Letters*. London: Dent, 1927.

Cassian, Abba. *The Sayings of the Desert Fathers*. Kalamazoo, MI: Cistercian, 1984.

The Catholic Source Book. Edited by Rev. Peter Klein. Dubuque: Brown-ROA, 1990.

Chrysostom, St. John. *Ecloga de oratione*. In *Catechism of the Catholic Church*, par. 2700. Saint Paul, MN: The Wanderer Press, 1994.

———. *Twelfth Homily on the Epistle to the Colossians*. In *The Four Cardinal Virtues*, by Josef Pieper. Notre Dame, IN: University of Notre Dame Press, 1966.

The Cloud of Unknowing. Garden City, NY: Image Books, 1973.

Desert Axiom. In *Spiritual Direction in the Early Christian East*, by Irénée Hausherr, translated by Anthony Gythiel. Kalamazoo, MI: Cistercian, 1990.

Doherty, Catherine. *Poustinia*. Combermere ON: Madonna House, 1993, 2000.

Dolan, Timothy Cardinal. "Rector's Conference on Penance." Lecture, Pontifical North American College, Rome. March 2, 1997.

Easter Exsultet. In the Roman Missal, 3rd ed.

Evagrius Ponticus. *The Praktikos & Chapters on Prayer*. Kalamazoo, MI: Cistercian, 1981.

Guillerand, Dom Augustin. *The Prayer of the Presence of God*. Manchester, NH: Sophia Institute Press, 2005.

Introduction to the Pentateuch. In *The New Jerusalem Bible*. Garden City, NY: Doubleday, 1985.

Irenaeus, St. *Against Heresies*. In *The Ante-Nicene Fathers*, vol. 1, edited by Rev. Alexander Roberts, D.D. Grand Rapids, MI: Eerdmans, 1979.

Isaiah the Monophysite. In *Spiritual Direction in the Early Christian East*, by Irénée Hausherr, translated by Anthony Gythiel. Kalamazoo, MI: Cistercian, 1990.

John of the Cross, St. *The Collected Works of Saint John of the Cross*. Translated by Kieran Kavanaugh, O.C.D., and Otilio Rodriguez, O.C.D. Washington, D.C.: Institute of Carmelite Studies, 1973.

John Paul II. *Crossing the Threshold of Hope*. UK: Random House, 1994.

———. *Veritatis splendor*. Vatican City: Libreria Editrice Vaticana, 1993.

Merry del Val, Rafael Cardinal. Litany of Humility.

Pieper, Joseph. *On Hope*. San Francisco: Ignatius Press, 1986.

Ravier, Andre, S.J. *Saint Bruno the Carthusian*. San Francisco: Ignatius Press, 1995.

Raymond of Capua. *Life of Catherine of Siena*. Translated by Conleth Kearns, O.P. Wilmington, DE: Glazier, 1980.

Sallust. *De coniuratione Catilinae*. In Encyclical Letter *Deus Caritas Est*, by Benedict XVI, par. 17.

Sequence of Pentecost. In the Roman Missal, 3rd ed.

Teresa of Calcutta, St. *Come Be My Light*. Edited by Brian Kolodiejchuk. New York, Doubleday, 2007.

Teresa of Ávila, St. *The Collected Works of Saint Teresa of Ávila*. 3 vols. Translated by Kieran Kavanaugh, O.C.D., and Otilio Rodriguez, O.C.D. Washington, D.C.: Institute of Carmelite Studies, 1987.

Thérèse of Lisieux, St. *Her Last Converations*. Translated by John Clarke, O.C.D. Washington, D.C.: Institute of Carmelite Studies, 1977.

———. *Story of a Soul*. 3rd ed. Translated by John Clarke, O.C.D. Washington, D.C.: Institute of Carmelite Studies, 1996.

William of Saint Thierry. *The Golden Epistle*. Translated by Theodore Berkeley. Kalamazoo, MI: Cistercian, 1980.

About the Author

Fr. Wayne Sattler is a diocesan priest in the diocese of Bismarck, ND. He also leads retreats on contemplative prayer based on the teachings of St. John of the Cross and St. Teresa of Ávila. Following God's call, Father lived as a diocesan hermit for six years, putting into practice the guidance of these two great mystics of the Church. During this time, he lived in a small cabin on an abandoned farmstead in rural North Dakota. It was in this solitude that the content of this book was undertaken. Fr. Sattler returned to his diocesan ministry in 2013 and now serves as the spiritual director in the diocese of Bismarck.

Sophia Institute

Sophia Institute is a nonprofit institution that seeks to nurture the spiritual, moral, and cultural life of souls and to spread the gospel of Christ in conformity with the authentic teachings of the Roman Catholic Church.

Sophia Institute Press fulfills this mission by offering translations, reprints, and new publications that afford readers a rich source of the enduring wisdom of mankind.

Sophia Institute also operates the popular online resource CatholicExchange.com. *Catholic Exchange* provides world news from a Catholic perspective as well as daily devotionals and articles that will help readers to grow in holiness and live a life consistent with the teachings of the Church.

In 2013, Sophia Institute launched Sophia Institute for Teachers to renew and rebuild Catholic culture through service to Catholic education. With the goal of nurturing the spiritual, moral, and cultural life of souls, and an abiding respect for the role and work of teachers, we strive to provide materials and programs that are at once enlightening to the mind and ennobling to the heart; faithful and complete, as well as useful and practical.

Sophia Institute gratefully recognizes the Solidarity Association for preserving and encouraging the growth of our apostolate over the course of many years. Without their generous and timely support, this book would not be in your hands.

www.SophiaInstitute.com
www.CatholicExchange.com
www.SophiaTeachers.org

Sophia Institute Press is a registered trademark of Sophia Institute.
Sophia Institute is a tax-exempt institution as defined by the
Internal Revenue Code, Section 501(c)(3). Tax ID 22-2548708.